"An alternative title for this book could have been *Billion-Dollar Wisdom* because that's what's inside. It's one thing to run a business for a year or two. It's an entirely different thing to lead a multibillion-dollar business for decades. Whether you've got a small team like me or a big dream of what could be, you'll always feel like you've underpaid for the amount of knowledge that's packed inside this book."

Jon Acuff, *New York Times* bestselling author of *Soundtracks*

"In my many years as a female CEO in the male-dominated trucking industry, I can testify that David Green's latest book, *Leadership Not by the Book*, is a refuge for those wanting to lead by God's Word and Holy Spirit and NOT by the ways of the world. I highly recommend this read for all leaders and aspiring leaders."

Marcia Taylor, CEO/Founder, Bennett Family of Companies

"I've written and spoken about God's Kingdom agenda as His visible manifestation of the comprehensive rule of God over every area of life. I can think of no better person than David Green to write about God's manifestation and the rule of God in the arena of business. This book, *Leadership Not by the Book*, is a must-read for those desiring to live by God's Kingdom agenda with their business, their ministry, and their leadership."

Dr. Tony Evans, president of The Urban Alternative, senior pastor of Oak Cliff Bible Fellowship

"Like David Green, I've learned by leading my own organization, Turning Point, that if you follow conventional wisdom, you'll land in conventional places. But if your leadership is by the Book and you are careful to obey, then you'll be amazed by the places God will take you. I highly recommend this read."

Dr. David Jeremiah, senior pastor, Shadow Mountain Community Church- El Cajon, CA, founder and CEO of Turning Point Ministries

"God often calls leaders to follow His guidance rather than traditions and trends—and my friend David Green is a prime example! In *Leadership Not by the Book*, David explains how leading by the

Good Book, the Bible, results in some unconventional decisions and surprising methods to exceed anything produced by human efforts alone. His fresh perspective and innovative insight make this book a must-read for every leader."

Chris Hodges, senior pastor of Church of the Highlands, author of *The Daniel Dilemma* and *Out of the Cave*

"For years, I've watched in awe at how Hobby Lobby, a store that's open only six days a week, has had astounding growth and success. The financial results have been remarkable, and from this insightful new book by my good friend David Green, you'll learn how this business achieved such incredible success. He shares everything you've ever wanted to know about one of the largest and most successful private companies in the United States. If you're ready to take your leadership and your business to the next level, this is the book for you!"

Robert Morris, senior pastor at Gateway Church, bestselling author of *The Blessed Life*, *Beyond Blessed*, and *Take the Day Off*

"In a day when there are leadership books written by those who never really successfully led an organization and church growth books written by those who never spent time pastoring a church, it is refreshing to discover this new volume by David Green with Bill High whose tried and true principles have actually been beaten out on the anvil of personal experience. This is a formula that works because it is God centered, people focused, and filled with commonsense application. In fact, across the years the Green family has been characterized by using common sense. But what sets them apart is that they also have the uncommon sense (faith) to believe God can still make the impossible possible. This is a book on leadership NOT by the book. And yet, at the same time, it is a volume on leadership by THE Book . . . of all books. Read it and reap!"

O. S. Hawkins PhD, former pastor of First Baptist Church in Dallas, President Emeritus of GuideStone Financial Resources, and bestselling author of The Code Series of devotionals with over two million sold

"If you want to learn the secret for successful significance, not just significant success, this book is a gold mine. The opposite of theory and convention, David shares the incredible story of scaling from unlikely startup to multibillion-dollar powerhouse with the decision points, principles, and leadership paradigms anyone is invited to live by. The world would be wrecked by the blessed wake that would result if business leaders read and heeded this invitation!"

Mike Sharrow, CEO, C12 Business Forums

"There are some people that when they talk, you listen. David Green is not only one of the most successful businesspeople on the planet, but he lives by a different code. He walks with godly wisdom in everything he does, and it sets him apart and gives him an authority. In *Leadership Not by the Book* he shares a lifetime of principles that have guided him. Some have helped him be unusually successful, and some have shaped his perspective to enjoy the journey a little bit more. In all of these, you will find pure gold advice that can dramatically change your own journey."

Matt Brown, evangelist, author of *Truth Plus Love*,
founder of Think Eternity

"If you look at the life of Christ, you will see that He turned traditional religious practices on their heads. He left the experts dumbfounded and changed eternity's entire narrative. In *Leadership Not by the Book*, David Green and Bill High take a lesson from Christ's way of life by turning traditional leadership upside down. Follow the practices found in this book, and your life as a leader in business, home, and faith will be transformed because you will no longer be conformed to the patterns of the world."

Rev. Samuel Rodriguez, president of NHCLC, author of
Persevere with Power, executive producer of Flamin' Hot

LEADERSHIP
Not BY
THE
BOOK

LEADERSHIP

Not BY THE BOOK

12 UNCONVENTIONAL PRINCIPLES TO DRIVE INCREDIBLE RESULTS

DAVID GREEN
WITH BILL HIGH

BakerBooks

a division of Baker Publishing Group
Grand Rapids, Michigan

Published by Baker Books
a division of Baker Publishing Group
PO Box 6287, Grand Rapids, MI 49516-6287
www.bakerbooks.com

Printed in the United States of America

Library of Congress Cataloging-in-Publication Data
Names: Green, David, 1941 November 13– author.
Title: Leadership not by the book : 12 unconventional principles to drive incredible results / David Green with Bill High.
Description: Grand Rapids, MI : Baker Books, a division of Baker Publishing Group, [2022] | Includes bibliographical references.
Identifiers: LCCN 2022012403 | ISBN 9781540902245 (cloth) | ISBN 9781493437771 (ebook)
Subjects: LCSH: Leadership—Moral and ethical aspects. | Business ethics. | Entrepreneurship—Moral and ethical aspects. | Hobby Lobby Creative Centers.
Classification: LCC HD57.7 .G733 2022 | DDC 658.4/092—dc23/eng/20220525
LC record available at https://lccn.loc.gov/2022012403

The proprietors are represented by the literary agency of A Drop of Ink, LLC.

Baker Publishing Group publications use paper produced from sustainable forestry practices and post-consumer waste whenever possible.

22   23   24   25   26   27   28   7   6   5   4   3   2   1

To all the leaders at Hobby Lobby
who helped form this book,
to the thousands of employees who
further our mission every day,
to the loyal customers who keep us going,
and to the love of my life, Barbara,
the very first person to run the business.

CONTENTS

INTRODUCTION

The Secret Sauce

It shouldn't work. So why does it?

Sometimes at Hobby Lobby, our customer service manager gives tours to corporate leaders. Some of them have graduated from business schools such as Harvard or other Ivy League colleges. He drives them around our premises in Oklahoma City on a golf cart. They go through our three warehouses, our art development rooms, our production and manufacturing lines, and our corporate offices. As he gives these tours, he hears our guests comment repeatedly, "Your operations fly in the face of everything we learned in business school. This is exactly the opposite of what we learned—but somehow it works."

We do things differently at Hobby Lobby, and leaders notice.

Like so many people, we started our business in our garage. Along the way, we had our moments of doubt whether we'd even make it. I'll be the first to admit, we learned much by trial and error. We've made plenty of mistakes over the years. But along the way, God has been gracious and guided us in ways that often haven't appeared to make sense. We weren't guided by business degrees, best practices, or focus groups. We didn't have a road map—just God, the Bible, prayer, and common sense. These are the ways we've watched Him work. And *as we followed Him*, we saw Him break the rules of traditional business practices and give us success.

When we started on this journey in 1970, we had no idea what lay ahead. We had no inkling of the sales trajectory God had planned for us:

1972: 1 store, $136.40 (August through December)

1982: 7 stores, $18 million

1992: 36 stores, $128 million

2002: 285 stores, $1.1 billion

2012: 520 stores, $3.3 billion

2022: 985 stores, $8 billion (projected)

In fifty years, we've gone from less than $150 to $8 billion in sales! Let me bear witness—that isn't me.

As we approach the fiftieth anniversary of Hobby Lobby, I'd like to look back and try to answer the question, Why does how we operate work when it shouldn't?

To begin, I know a few things for sure:

- It isn't merely a success formula.
- It doesn't only reflect sound business practices.

- It isn't dumb luck.
- And it *certainly* isn't a result of any extraordinary foresight or ability on my part.

And yet, God has used me to help create an $8 billion a year business that employs more than fifty thousand men and women across the country. He's enabled us to give away 50 percent of our profits to help fund remarkably effective initiatives for His kingdom all over the world. It has been a wonderfully satisfying, thrilling, scary, eye-opening, perplexing, enjoyable ride lasting half a century!

But really, none of this is what interests me the most. I find the following question far more exciting: What if God might want to use *you* to do a new, even greater work?

While we celebrate what God has done so far through Hobby Lobby and our associated companies, I'm praying that the Lord will raise up hundreds, thousands, maybe tens of thousands of talented leaders—whether in business or ministry—with hearts committed to Christ. I dream of an army of men and women who want to not only create successful organizations but also use those enterprises to make a difference for Jesus around the world. Keep in mind that I believe the unconventional principles discussed in this book apply whether you lead a business, a church, a nonprofit, or are just contemplating the idea of leadership.

I want to lay out for you the core elements that have enabled Hobby Lobby to thrive, even though to many observers our success has seemed not just improbable but impossible. Much of our success, frankly, *is* improbable from a merely human standpoint. But we have never pursued business from a merely human standpoint.

We always take care to describe success in terms of what God has done. That, in fact, is a crucial part of our *secret sauce*, which I want to describe for you. I would love for this sauce, or some version of it, to become your own, enabling you to reach heights you've never even dreamed of achieving. God rarely chooses to duplicate what He's already done. What new thing might He want to do through *you*?

The Secret Sauce

Every secret sauce includes many ingredients, and the amount and combination of these ingredients give each sauce its unique flavor. While every ingredient plays a key role in the sauce's essence, some ingredients play far more critical roles than others.

As I highlight the ingredients that make up the secret sauce responsible for the success of Hobby Lobby, it might help to place those ingredients in three major categories:

1. God-centered practices
2. People-focused practices
3. Commonsense practices

While each of the ingredients we'll consider has proven critical to Hobby Lobby's success, some ingredients have played (and continue to play) an outsized role in our growth. We could not have expanded from a family business that began with a $600 loan in 1970 to a contemporary company with 985 stores nationwide, stocking 100,000 items, without this secret sauce.

I realize that most corporations with priceless secret recipes zealously guard their proprietary formulations, often keeping them locked up in high-security vaults. I think of the carefully protected recipes for Coca-Cola, KFC, Dr Pepper, or Bush's Baked Beans. By contrast, I am handing you the secret sauce that powers Hobby Lobby. Why?

First, it's not really mine to hang on to. While the Lord used me to establish and lead Hobby Lobby, it's His company, not mine. He made that clear to me several years ago when I wondered what I should do about company succession and ownership. It's one of the secret ingredients you'll read about.

Second, I'd like to see countless men and women around the globe use this secret sauce to create their own, very different versions, suitable for a wide variety of industries, businesses, ministries, and nonprofits—not to enrich themselves but to give millions of families stable incomes and enjoyable, meaningful places to work. Beyond that, I long to see them create such high-performing organizations that they gain the means to fund or build new, extraordinary initiatives for God's kingdom from one corner of the earth to the other, blessing those made in God's image wherever they may live under God's heaven.

The Most Important Question

Why does Hobby Lobby work when it really shouldn't? What's the secret sauce that makes it all possible? As intriguing and helpful as I think the answers to these questions are, the most important question is one only you can answer: *How may God want to use you to create some new sensation (one that "just shouldn't work," but does) to bring life to families, blessing to the world, and joy to God's heart?*

That's the story I'm looking forward to hearing as you apply the principles in this book.

PART ONE

GOD-FOCUSED PRACTICES

one

GIVE THE TRUE OWNER THE VOTE

At several crucial times in my life, God has seized my attention in unforgettable ways to alter my path and to change how we do things at Hobby Lobby. Each of these pivotal episodes resulted in some paradigm shift, a few of them larger than others. We wouldn't be where we are today without them.

I never saw any of them coming. I didn't always immediately understand their meaning or significance. And more than once they rocked me out of some unhelpful pattern before they filled me with gratitude and delight over some new thing God wanted to do in, with, and through us.

Out of a handful of such experiences, three stand out as catalysts for major change. Although they took place many years apart, they've worked together in my life to transform the way I think and act as a leader. They also continue to teach me that God is amazingly patient with us, always desiring our best but never hesitant to point out traits, beliefs, actions, or habits that *really* need to go. And typically, only when they do go does He set things in motion to give us the success He's had in mind all along.

The First Catalyst for Change

Hobby Lobby has grown slowly over the years. By the time we reach our fiftieth anniversary in August 2022, we expect to operate about a thousand stores with combined yearly sales of around $8 billion.

Things looked much different back in 1979 when we had only four stores with sales less than .002 percent of today's sales. We were "succeeding" but just barely. My wife, Barbara, and I gave 10 percent of our personal earnings to God's work, but at that point the company made no corporate donations. I figured we needed to plow all excess funds back into Hobby Lobby to help it continue to grow. I hoped that, one day, we might become strong enough corporately to start giving a small percentage of our profits to worthy ministries. Someday.

On a flight home after attending that year's denominational convention of our church, I sat next to a window. As I looked out at the clouds and to the ground far below, I suddenly sensed the Lord speaking to my heart: *You need to give $30,000 for Bible literature.*

A missionary's words delivered at the conference, describing an acute need for such literature, quickly came to mind—but what did that have to do with me? We had only a handful of stores, none of them setting sales records. How could we afford to give away $30,000? *That's impossible*, I thought.

But as I sat by that window and prayed about what I thought I heard the Spirit say to me, another idea hit: *What if we gave $7,500, four times? We could write four checks and postdate them a month apart for four months.* The latter seemed far more doable than giving thirty grand outright, but was it just a crazy idea?

When I returned home, I described my plane episode to Barbara and told her about my idea. We discussed it, prayed about it, and eventually decided to go for it. We wrote the checks and put them in the mail, along with an explanatory letter. Several days later, we received a phone call from a denominational official who had received our little package. He informed us that four African missionaries had held a special prayer meeting to ask for literature funds *on the very day we had postmarked our letter.* "Looks like God answered their prayer!" he added.

The checks were deposited according to our instructions, and they didn't bounce. So began our corporate giving (something I'll describe in more detail a bit later). In fact though, the episode played a much bigger role in my life and thinking than merely initiating our corporate giving.

My parents and my five siblings had all gone into church ministry of one kind or another. I was the only one who had not. For years, I felt like something of a black sheep. You know, the only one in the family to go astray, the lone ne'er-do-well who chose to wander off into the wasteland of business.

Not long after Barbara and I gave our "impossible" amount, it struck me that God had called me into business just as surely as He had called my family members into church ministry. God had a definite purpose for me in my work as a Christian businessman! The Lord wanted to use what I did in my company to expand His kingdom. The idea both surprised and thrilled me.

I've written this book, in part, to encourage you to adopt the same understanding. God wants to use your business, your company, your organization, your group for kingdom purposes. I don't know how; that's for you to discover. But I do know He has a definite purpose for you to fulfill, one that fits somewhere in His ongoing mission to this world.

Despite this pivotal incident, however, I didn't yet think of our company as a ministry. That realization would come much later and would require at least two more divine episodes. I did, however, start walking toward a destination *very* different from the one I had in mind when I began.

The Second Catalyst for Change

Hobby Lobby saw steady growth from the late 1970s to the mid-1980s. We opened more stores and earned tens of millions in annual sales. The future looked fantastic. I even began to suspect that I might be a genius.

And then came 1985.

This time, God didn't speak to me as I sat by an airplane window. I didn't hear from Him while flying thirty thousand feet above the ground. On this occasion, I heard from Him while huddled under my big mahogany desk with my office door closed, desperately praying. I left my phone unanswered because I already knew the callers: creditors demanding we pay bills we couldn't pay. The underside of my desk became my refuge.

What had happened in six years?

During the Oklahoma oil boom of the 1980s, I had overextended us. I bought inventory on credit, assuming the money would keep rolling in. Then the oil bust hit, the economy tanked, and the bank threatened to foreclose on us. Every time I tried to fix the problem, my brilliant solution backfired. I tried to save money wherever I could, but we lost money on sales because our stores didn't have the merchandise they needed. For the first time in the history of our company, we landed in red ink, a wide sea of it. By the end of 1985, we had lost nearly $1 million, more than any two years of profit we'd ever earned.

Under my desk, I turned to the only place I knew to go. I turned to God. I felt Him saying to my heart: *If you're so big, I'm going to let you have it by yourself.*

I was a proud man. I had grown cocky from all my success. I imagined that I had the Midas touch, that I had become an Einstein of business. Ever since I worked retail in high school, I had stampeded through the ranks, becoming the youngest store manager, the youngest district manager, the first in charge of a prototype store. Finally, I started my own company. Every year from 1972 to 1985, Hobby Lobby turned a profit.

I assumed the gravy train would last forever, and so I took on more and more debt. I allowed myself to get a big head—and God temporarily removed His blessing. Oh, He still provided for me. He gave me life. He gave me breath. But He stopped giving us what our company most needed—His blessing.

If you've ever thought, *David Green is so smart*, then let me shatter your delusion. All by itself, 1985 proved to me that I'm not so smart. Without God's help, I couldn't sustain even a dozen stores, much less a thousand.

In April 1986 I called a family meeting to describe how very serious our predicament had become. With my pride shattered, I tearfully admitted that I didn't know what to do. Mart, my oldest son (then twenty-four years old), replied, "Dad, it's okay. Our faith is not in you—it's in God. If we lose the businesses, we'll still be okay." I started to breathe a little.

God must destroy our arrogant pride if He is to bless the work of our hands. The Lord loves to bless humility, not smug self-confidence. It's hard to maintain a smug self-confidence when you're crouching under your desk, hiding from creditors, and pleading for God to help you out of the mess you've created for yourself! Today, I can say I'm glad for those dark days. I needed to have my bubble burst.

I needed a good dose of reality that would prompt me to say, along with another leader who centuries before had experienced God's fierce opposition to human pride: "I . . . praise and exalt and glorify the King of heaven, because everything he does is right and all his ways are just. And those who walk in pride he is able to humble" (Dan. 4:37).

Once I humbled myself, the Lord again blessed the work of Hobby Lobby. The economy picked up, we made some adjustments, and by the end of 1986, the company became profitable once more. By God's grace, it has managed to remain in the black every year since then.

This episode also taught me an important secondary lesson. Through it, the Lord led us to get rid of our long-term debt (see chapter 3). For now, I'll say that accumulating long-term debt implies that we know what the future will bring when only God knows what lies ahead. He forcefully clarified *that* truth for me through my season of desk diving.

The Third Catalyst for Change

So far, so good. God first taught me that He had called me into business for a divine purpose. Then He reminded me that any success we enjoy comes ultimately from His grace and provision and that He always opposes human pride. About fifteen years after my second lesson, I was ready for the third.

Hobby Lobby survived its mid-1980s scare and by the late 1990s had grown to around two hundred stores and was approaching $1 billion in yearly sales. By that time, a very different set of troubles began to cost me a lot of sleep.

How would we handle the twin questions of inheritance and succession? What would happen to my grandchildren, great-grandchildren, and more distant heirs if they should become millionaires even before they were born? And who would take over the leadership of Hobby Lobby when I stepped down as CEO? How would we make those crucial decisions? These issues kept me awake night after night.

One evening while praying in my backyard about these agonizing decisions, I sensed the Lord asking me, *What would happen if the Jones family owned this and you were just the CEO?*

"I'd have nothing to give," I answered.

At that moment, I recognized that if I claimed God owned Hobby Lobby—something I had repeated for years—I couldn't continue to act as though it belonged to me. In fact, Hobby Lobby was not mine, either to command or to give away.

For decades I had insisted, like many Christians, that God owned the company we built. And yet, that night I had to admit that I didn't even *remotely* understand what divine ownership involved. What did it mean, in a practical, hands-on sense that God owned Hobby Lobby? I started asking myself, *Am I handling the issues of succession and inheritance any differently than would a completely secular leader would?*

My uncomfortable question drove me to think more deeply about two critical issues:

1. What does it mean that God owns Hobby Lobby?
2. If God owns Hobby Lobby, then how do we operate differently than those who believe they own their businesses?

I started looking into God's Word for answers, and I quickly found the Lord's response to my first question.

Does God *Really* Own Everything?

The Bible couldn't be more emphatic on this issue. In verse after verse and Scripture after Scripture, it tells us that the God who created everything also owns everything.

The Word of God insists, "The earth is the LORD's, and everything in it, the world, and all who live in it" (Ps. 24:1). No exceptions. No caveats. David likewise prays, "Yours, LORD, is the greatness and the power and the glory and the majesty and the splendor, for everything in heaven and earth is yours" (1 Chron. 29:11).

Just before the Israelites entered the promised land, Moses warned them, "You may say to yourself, 'My power and the strength of my hands have produced this wealth for me.' But remember the LORD your God, for it is he who gives you the ability to produce wealth, and so confirms his covenant, which he swore to your ancestors, as it is today" (Deut. 8:17–18).

Has your power produced wealth for you? Has the strength of your hands created a thriving company? Moses would tell you, "You have what you do only because God gave you the ability to generate wealth."

In fact, *everything* belongs to God. Wealth comes from Him and belongs to Him. None of us owns anything, whether we admit it or not. God owns it all.

Stewardship versus Ownership

If we don't own the companies and organizations that God has enabled us to create, then how are we to manage them? If we're not owners, then what are we?

The Bible would answer, "You're stewards."[1] You carefully manage the resources and property that belong to someone else—namely, God. I have discovered that every one of the vexing problems ownership created for me, stewardship has resolved.

When we acted as though we owned Hobby Lobby, we thought the company owed us. When we started viewing Hobby Lobby as God's, we realized that we owe the company. We now see Hobby Lobby as a ministry whose mission God calls us to further through our service. We are stewards, not owners.

When you're an owner, wealth can easily become a curse. When you're a steward, wealth becomes a tool.

When family members see themselves as stewards, they don't feel entitled to wealth. Unlike owners, they know they must earn their income through their labor.

When you're not the owner, you're just one among equals. As a steward, you're not the elephant in the room.

It's a hundred times better to be a steward of a company than to have to worry about how to handle ownership and who gets what after you die! Recognizing that God owns Hobby Lobby solved every one of my troubles with succession, inheritance, and operations. (If you would like the short version of how we handled these things, see appendix A.) But more than that, it set us up to make an outsized difference in this world that otherwise would have been impossible.

Give God the Vote

Leading as a steward of God's resources requires divine wisdom. Just because you *can* do something as the leader doesn't mean you *should*. Power can cause great damage when handled poorly—and a lot of power can cause a lot of damage.

Because God owns Hobby Lobby, I have learned to give God the vote in all major decisions. For those big decisions, I hit pause and set up the decision in a way that gives God the final vote.

I first saw how this could work through the example of a man named Gideon who lived a long time ago. He needed to make sure that it was God who had called him into battle against a huge enemy army. If God hadn't instructed him to send his men into the conflict, he wouldn't dare to put his soldiers' lives on the line since it looked like a hopeless cause. He asked God for a sign of confirmation, and God gave it to him (Judg. 6). We often call such a request a *fleece*, recalling the unlikely nature of the sign Gideon requested. Gideon moved forward and won a great victory.

I've learned to do a similar thing when I face a big decision regarding some situation about which the Bible appears to give me no clear guidance. First, I pray about it and ask God to show me what to do. If I'm still unsure, I "put out a fleece" as Gideon did. I structure my requested outcome in a way that seems extremely unlikely. I stack the cards against myself, if you will. That way, if it happens, I take it as God's answer that He wanted it to take place. If it doesn't happen, I take it as God's no.

One time a company came up for sale that Hobby Lobby had an interest in acquiring. I prayed about it, still felt unsure about what to do, and then offered an amount below what my CFO told me the company was worth. We didn't get the company. Now, I had seen God do the miraculous enough times to know that if He had wanted us to have that company, we could have purchased it at the lower price. But God voted no, and I trust that He had reasons for His choice that I know nothing about (and may never know until heaven).

If God owns your company and you give Him the vote, you must accept whatever He says, both when He replies yes and when He answers no. However He votes, you must receive that answer as your marching orders.

What big decisions do you face right now that may call for giving God the vote? How can you structure your prayer request to make it plain that God says to you either "Go for it" or "Don't take another step"? Keep in mind that the obvious choice may not be the right choice. What does God think? That's the important question.

You're wise if you wait to let God have a say in the matter. What a sense of assurance you can enjoy when you really believe that God is in the very middle of running your (His) business!

God Must Lead

It's easy to say that God is in charge and that He owns the business. But when things go in a different direction from what we want, what happens then? Too often, we act as though we're in charge. The question is, How does God vote in your business, your organization, your ministry? In what way is God really in charge? How is He truly the owner? If you want to create some new initiative designed to bless the world, you can't omit this crucial element.

When we were less than half the size we are now, I went out to the warehouse one day feeling crazy confused about how to move ahead. Everything seemed extremely complex. In a large, nationwide company, you have a million things to think about. I sat down and prayed, "God, I don't know what to do."

In response to my prayer, over a period of about two weeks the Lord led me to what we should do and not do. He showed me we were doing a lot of things we shouldn't have been doing.

We were selling some items at 40 percent off, for example, when we could have sold just as many at regular price. We changed our ad—and our sales volume almost immediately jumped. We took in extra sales because we listened to the Lord. God helped me and gave me insight after I confessed, "This is too big for me."

And He'll help you too.

No Need to Worry

Randy Alcorn, author of the excellent book *Managing God's Money*, relates a story from the seventeenth century. A frantic man rode his horse wildly up to the famous evangelist and preacher John Wesley. "Mr. Wesley, Mr. Wesley," he shouted, "something terrible has happened! Your house has burned to the ground!"

Wesley thought a moment and then replied, "No. The Lord's house burned to the ground. That means one less responsibility for me."

Wesley's outlook is a key ingredient of the secret sauce that has allowed Hobby Lobby to thrive. Alcorn says about Wesley's response to his house burning down: "We might say, 'Get real,' but Wesley's reaction didn't stem from a denial of reality. Rather, it sprang from life's most basic reality—that God is the owner of all things, and we are simply his stewards."[2]

Do you see yourself as a steward or as an owner? Test yourself. How do you think you would react if your business, organization, or ministry burned to the ground tonight?

TWO

LISTEN TO AND OBEY THE HOLY SPIRIT ABOVE ALL

Where were you in March 2020, the month COVID shut down the world? Airport hallways grew empty as passengers stopped booking flights. Teachers told students to bring textbooks home over spring break in case they couldn't return. It seemed the world had started falling apart, and no one knew what to do. The unexpected crashed around us, testing every leader.

At Hobby Lobby, we first shut down nineteen stores in Pennsylvania. My wife and I thought, *We'll just keep paying those employees even while the stores are closed.*

As more and more stores closed, we started wondering, *How will we take care of our employees? How will we survive as a business?* We asked the same questions nearly every other business owner asked. As things worsened day by day, we took the only route we knew—prayer.

Stuck at home, Barbara and I came together for prayer every morning, noon, and evening. We knelt in our living room and asked God, "What should we do?"

Early in the pandemic, Barbara sensed that God gave her three words: *guide*, *guard*, and *groom*. She took these words as assurance that God remained in control and that the pandemic would not ultimately hurt us or Hobby Lobby. God would guide our company and family. He would guard us. And He would use the hard times to groom us, to refine what He didn't like in order to make us even more like Him. Those three words brought great comfort to us and to our family as the situation continued to deteriorate.

By the end of April, we had to shut down every Hobby Lobby store in America. As we watched revenue drop to zero, it became apparent that we couldn't keep paying all our employees. We had to furlough the majority of our staff. I'm grateful that the government stepped in to provide unemployment to those without work. As we watched a nation shut down, we wondered what would happen next.

In May and June, some states began relaxing their shelter-in-place orders and we started reopening stores. We kept flexing according to ever-changing governmental mandates, but we opened where we could. And somehow, we watched sales increase.

By July, sales had jumped back to the same level they had reached the year before. We breathed a sigh of relief.

But then, something truly strange happened. Sales *sky-rocketed*. August, September, October—each month surpassed our sales from the year before. Since our supply chain remained as backed up as ever, I wondered what our stores even had to sell. We had a hard time keeping our shelves stocked during the pandemic. Anything we had expected from overseas remained on hold as other countries suffered even tighter lockdowns. The stock on our warehouse shelves grew ever sparser. How could we ship items we didn't have to stores we barely kept open?

And yet, merchandise kept flying off the shelves. It made no sense.

When the Christmas season approached, we had only 60 percent of our normal inventory—and yet, sales kept rising. *What are our customers buying?* we wondered. When inventory goes down, sales should too, but they didn't. Our sales soared higher than ever!

Incredibly, 2020 turned into the highest sales year Hobby Lobby had ever seen. We ended that year with 50 percent greater growth than the year before. But how? Such growth is unheard of in normal years, much less in a pandemic when stores shut down and merchandise remains on ships.

At the end of the year, we compared ourselves to other craft stores that sold the same items we did. Many consumers did simply stay at home and work on more crafts. Puzzles, clay molding, art supplies, and other craft items sold well. But if that alone explained our growth, then our competitors should have seen the same growth. They didn't. Only Hobby Lobby saw overall sales growth despite the shutdown. Our competitors' sales dropped, ending 2020 in the same or worse condition than the year before.

Now, does that make sense? How could we sell the *same* items yet be the only craft store to see significant sales growth? Something else clearly was going on.

In early 2021, I gathered my staff and reported the remarkable sales we had experienced the year before. We celebrated! But I also explained that although we sold the same merchandise as our competitors, we alone had seen growth in sales. How could that happen?

I believe it happened because God answered our prayers by His grace. We deserved *no* credit for this. Our smarts didn't earn it. God alone deserved all the glory for this remarkable blessing.

If you are a business or organizational leader with a heart committed to Christ who wants to impact this world for God, leaning on the Holy Spirit must become second nature to you. You must learn to listen for God's voice and then obey whatever He tells you. With that potent ingredient in the mix, the sauce you create can fuel some spectacular results.

Pray to an Ever-Present God

Three extraordinary Bible verses help me to know how to pray in both good times and bad. The first verse tells me,

"Pray without ceasing" (1 Thess. 5:17 KJV). God wants us to pray, always. He never gets tired of hearing our voices. Every instant is the best time to pray. There never comes a time to stop praying.

In the second verse, God promises, "Never will I leave you; never will I forsake you" (Heb. 13:5). If the Lord never leaves me, that means He's always with me. I picture Jesus right beside me—all the time. Whether I'm at work, at home, or wherever, He is there. He's not someplace "out there" far away; He is right here next to me.

I combine these two verses to get a picture of how God wants us to walk with Him every day. If someone remained right next to you all day, wouldn't it make sense to talk to them throughout the day? It would get a little awkward if you ignored them. God wants us to pray continually because He is with us continually, including right now. As you read these words, He is beside you. He never leaves you, and He never forsakes you. You can talk to him continually and know that He hears you.

Every day without exception, you and I need direction. Little problems pop up daily in our families, our marriages, and our work. Big problems also crash into our lives unannounced. Because Jesus is ever present with us, He wants to be involved in every decision, big and small. This is the pathway to collaborating with God on world-changing ventures.

Every day, I try to walk with the understanding that He is with me all the time. I invite Him to guide me in all the decisions I must make each day. I attempt to have a constant conversation with Him. I run ideas by Him. And if I'm not sure what to do, I wait. I leave room for Him to speak to me in His time. He always does.

Never Too Late

In 2007 I sensed the Lord directing me to hire our current director of management ministries, Debbie Kinsey. I didn't realize how miraculous this was until I later heard her side of the story.

Debbie and her husband lived in Tulsa until he accepted a pastoral position at our church in Oklahoma City. She worked at a college in Tulsa, and once her husband accepted the new position, she began looking for education jobs in Oklahoma City. However, a hiring freeze in education meant she found nothing. But God spoke to her heart and instructed her to quit her job. She told her husband, and he agreed that she should resign. She did so and moved with him to Oklahoma City, not knowing where she would work.

Soon after she arrived, God spoke to her again, laying a date on her heart and saying, *By this date, you will have a job.* It felt so clear to her that she went to her calendar and marked the date: one month later, on a Wednesday.

Until then, she kept applying for jobs and interviewing, but no one offered her anything. The day she had marked on her calendar arrived with no job in sight. When the clock ticked to 5:00 p.m., she gave up hope. The church had scheduled her to speak that night, but she really didn't want to go. She thought she had heard so clearly from

God. She went to church anyway, discouraged, but still delivered the message.

After the service, I asked to speak with her.

"I don't know if we've officially met, but I'm David Green," I told her. We chatted a minute, and then I said, "I have been praying. Thirty days ago, God laid you on my heart to offer you a position."

I had no idea *that* day was the very one she had circled on her calendar! I didn't yet know exactly what her role would be, but I knew God wanted her to work for us. After she told me her story, it became clear that God had spoken to both of us.

Most books on business insist on keeping God out of the decision-making process. The secular world considers it unprofessional and even foolish to make decisions just because God somehow spoke to us. But if our God really is the all-knowing Creator, and if He loves us, then wouldn't it make sense for us to ask Him what to do? If He knows everything and loves us enough to send His Son to die for us, how foolish, unprofessional, and wrong would it be *not* to invite Him into every decision?

You Have Not Because You Ask Not

The third verse that helps me know how to pray is James 4:2: "You do not have because you do not ask God." Time and again throughout my career, God has miraculously answered prayer. He speaks to us, and He wants us to come to Him with our requests.

In the early 1980s, an oil boom in Oklahoma improved business for practically everyone in our state. Customers had extra cash to spend, which meant more purchases. The downside was that oil companies began hiring like crazy. Hobby Lobby saw some of our best employees in the IT department leave to work for this or that oil company.

I knew God wants us to go to Him in everything. I also knew God loves the people running the oil companies as much as He loves me. He has no favorites. So I drove to an oil company's facilities, got out of my car, and walked around the premises, praying about the situation and asking God to bless both Hobby Lobby and that oil company.

From that day on, we stopped losing our best people.

God cares about our problems. He cares about employee retention. "You do not have because you do not ask," He says. He wants us to ask. He wants to grow our faith. He also knows (and wants us to realize) that we're not as smart as we think we are. Only when we start listening to what God says do we begin to see results.

More recently, I had to trust God when our supply chain once more got backed up during the coronavirus outbreak. By July 2021, we should have received our fall merchandise, but we hadn't. A port in China had closed because of the virus while other stops along the way had fewer staff than usual. Again, I started praying.

Jesus never needs reminding, of course, but I said to Him, "Your disciples twice fished unsuccessfully all night long. You solved their problem both times. You told them what to do, and they did it. God, this freight is all clogged up. Please release it. You did it for the disciples, and You can do it for us."

In the following weeks, I watched as truck after truck of freight arrived at our warehouse. I counted fifteen trucks one morning. Every time I saw one, I prayed, "Thank You, Lord!" Every truck felt like an answered prayer.

Would you like to see remarkable answered prayers like these in your own business or organization? You can if you will listen to and obey the Holy Spirit. Perhaps God is waiting right now to hear from you so that He can create some new sensation in your own world.

Many have told me of amazing answered prayers. One day Debbie was speaking with a manager of a store located in a city near the Canadian border. He didn't know what to do about his struggling store.

"I've tried everything," he confided, "and our sales aren't increasing." His town's population simply didn't provide enough foot traffic for his store to thrive.

"All you can do is your best," Debbie tried to encourage him, "and sometimes things still just don't work out." As they began winding down their conversation, she prayed for him. At the end of her prayer, before she thought about what she was saying, she blurted out, "God, he needs customers. Please send customers to his store."

The next day, the excited manager called her. "You're not going to believe this!" he said. "A whole busload of senior citizen Canadian women came here to shop for the day. I'm on my way to pick up donuts for them while they shop!"

God Will Strengthen You

No matter your line of work, regardless of what you are going through, God wants to be involved in every aspect of your life. His Word promises, "For the eyes of the LORD range throughout the earth to strengthen those whose hearts are fully committed to him" (2 Chron. 16:9). He wants to strengthen you, and He will guide and direct you.

One of our family's hardest trials occurred in 2014 when we reluctantly took the US government to court. The Health and Human Services Department under President Obama had issued a mandate that would have required Hobby Lobby to provide and facilitate four potentially life-terminating drugs and devices in our health insurance plan. In layman's terms, it would have forced us either to pay for abortions or to pay severe daily fines for noncompliance. The case eventually worked its way up to the Supreme Court. We and our legal team appeared before the court in March 2014 to argue that individuals do not lose their religious freedom when they open a family business.

We didn't know what the outcome would be or whether our business would come out alive on the other side. We had surrendered Hobby Lobby to God and knew He was in control, but the waiting period felt excruciating. Our employees also felt the weight of the situation, especially our senior leadership. But in the ordeal, we saw God strengthen not only our faith but also the faith of our employees. We knew people across the nation were praying for Hobby Lobby and for our family, and we experienced

God speaking miraculously not only to us but also to our colleagues.

While in Washington, DC, for the hearing, our general counsel, Peter Dobelbower, and his wife went out to tour the city. They took a Sunday taxi ride to a museum. At the end of the ride, their Nigerian driver handed them a receipt along with a card that asked, Do you know Jesus?

The note surprised Peter, and he replied, "Yes, thank you, we do." Peter then added, "I'd like to ask you to pray for me. I am with Hobby—" The driver cut him off midsentence.

"Yes, I know who you are," the man said. "This is your divine appointment, and you will win."

"What?"

"This is your divine appointment," the driver repeated, "and you will win."

Peter and his wife sat in the back seat, crying. They could hardly believe that God sent a Nigerian taxi driver to encourage them before our court appearance. They thanked the man and went on their way. Peter told us the story, and we all carried that assurance with us into court the next day. Sure enough, by God's grace, three months later, on June 30, the Supreme Court ruled 5–4 in favor of Hobby Lobby. We consider it a victory for all who seek to live out their faith.

Sometimes God sends us a divine word as He did that day to Peter through the taxi driver. But often He simply provides the gentle assurance of peace as we pray about whatever concerns us. Faith doesn't mean trusting God only in the easy times. It means trusting God always, no matter the situation, whether in sunshine or storms.

A Different Route

As a leader, have you ever thought, *This makes no sense! What am I doing here? This can't be the way. Surely, I've gotten it wrong. There must be another route! This is too hard.*

Doubts creep in, whether you've just started or are a seasoned leader. When the rug gets pulled out from under you and unexpected developments change everything, when things don't make sense, you want at least plain road signs that point the way. You want straight paths. "Just give me the map, God, and I'll take it from here."

Instead, we have a God who sometimes leads us to the edge of the sea. Psalm 77:19 says, "Your path led through the sea, your way through the mighty waters, though your footprints were not seen."

When the ancient Israelites fled Egypt, God led them to the promised land but not by the route that made the most apparent sense. Most travelers would have gone straight north and crossed a river instead of a sea.

But God knew what they didn't know. He knew that if the Israelites took the usual route, they would have had to cross enemy territory and start fighting battles they weren't yet equipped to fight. Their young faith couldn't handle such a challenge. So instead of taking the way that made apparent sense, He led them straight to the edge of an impassible sea.

As they stood at the shoreline, gazing at an endless expanse of water that met sky in the distant horizon, they had to wonder what God was doing. Surely *this* couldn't be the right way. It made no sense, especially with a huge army of angry Egyptians hot on their tails. With the depths in front of them and a pursuing army behind them, what could they do, other than die?

But God had a plan. He told Moses to raise his staff and stretch his hand over the water, "and all that night the LORD drove the sea back with a strong east wind and turned it into dry land. The waters were divided, and the Israelites went through the sea on dry ground, with a wall of water on their right and on their left" (Exod. 14:21–22).

We often have no way of knowing what will happen. We have no solutions. We have no formulas. And yet God comes through for us, time after time after time.

A Test to Pass

We obey God not because of what we will get but because He deserves our obedience. The Bible praises Abraham for his faith, which he proved through obedience even though he thought it would cost him everything. When God asked Abraham to sacrifice his only son, Abraham packed up some firewood and took Isaac on a journey, fully intending to obey (Gen. 22).

Of course, God had no desire for Abraham to kill his son. The Lord quickly provided another sacrifice instead. But God did test Abraham to see if he would willingly give up that which he loved the most. Abraham listened to God and obeyed Him, and God honored him for it.

God wants us to obey Him in times of blessing and in times of testing. This means doing the right thing no matter the cost, even if we believe we'll lose money, influence, or exciting opportunities.

I'm not proud to admit it, but God had to deal with me longer than He should have regarding our selling of Halloween items. I loved Halloween as a kid. We never had much candy (or anything else) growing up, so Halloween excited me. I beat every other kid to the street and was the last one to go home. I saw it as my one chance to stock up on candy for the season.

When the company first decided whether we would carry Halloween merchandise, I said, "Why not? We celebrated Halloween as preacher's kids, so what could be wrong with it?" In time, however, God convicted me that the current expression of the holiday did not honor Him. Hobby Lobby last carried Halloween merchandise in 2019, when God put it on my heart to discontinue it. Did I believe the decision would cost us a lot of money? Yes. Was it the right thing to do? Yes.

The Lord doesn't necessarily lead all of us to the same convictions on every issue; each of us must listen to God for ourselves. But God emphatically *does* speak to us on specific issues. The question is whether we will obey, regardless of the result. Such decisions may look like they'll cost us in the short run, but I have seen that they usually pay off in the long run.

I had assumed our decision to stop carrying Halloween items would cost us millions of dollars in profit, but as I've mentioned, we had our highest sales ever in 2020. And that, despite a pandemic that temporarily shut down all our stores.

God blesses us when we hear and obey.

More than anything, God wants to see our faith grow. It means far more to Him than millions in profits or billions in sales. How could we think that the One who made everything in the universe somehow feels the tiniest bit impressed with the size or profitability of our little business ventures or other initiatives? God wants us to listen to Him and obey Him, no matter what it might cost or how risky it may seem.

Whatever your leadership role, are you listening to the Holy Spirit? Are you allowing the people on your team to listen to Him as well? If you want to bless the world through your work, make prayer a priority.

THRee

GIVE AWAY
YOUR PROFIT

No doubt you've heard the saying "Profit above all else." Common business practice typically sees profit as paramount. A business exists to make money, right?

But the Bible answers that question in this way: "Cast but a glance at riches, and they are gone, for they will surely sprout wings and fly off to the sky like an eagle" (Prov. 23:5). If your only goal is making a profit, you are stuck with only short-term gains.

God tells us that caring for others, especially the poor and marginalized, is one of the best ways to truly live out our faith. Building schools, starting businesses, improving agricultural techniques, providing clean water—all of these provide better education, better economies, better food sources, and better health services for thousands of precious men and women made in God's image. Wherever we can, along with supplying these services, we also offer the lifesaving news of God's love for every person. Part of the 50 percent of our company profit that we give away each year goes to fund exactly these kinds of initiatives.

Why Give 50 Percent?

This world has nothing more that I want. *Nothing*. I already have everything I need.

Even though Hobby Lobby became far more profitable after we started to give more, I still make the same salary as before. I have not taken a raise in sixteen years. I make 5 percent of what most CEOs do.

What would I do with more money? Buy a second house? The one I have now gives me more than enough problems. One house is plenty.

I watch CEOs make more and more money so that they can buy a boat, a vacation home, a private island—I can't imagine any of those things giving Barbara and me more than thirty minutes of happiness. I have no desire whatever to have more of this world's goods. Stuff is just stuff, nothing more. It's empty.

Giving away half of Hobby Lobby's profit also attracts and motivates great employees. Many individuals come to work for Hobby Lobby because they feel inspired by our mission. They stay motivated as they continue to see how their work makes a difference around the world.

Giving away profit gives me greater joy than anything money could buy. Even better, it passes along the same joy to our employees. And most of all, it allows us to partner with God in what He's doing around the world. As the old ad said, "Try it, you'll like it!"

How We Got to 50 Percent

A few years after we founded Hobby Lobby, we started tithing our profits, giving 10 percent to various charities. Whatever we made one year, we took 10 percent and gave it away the following year. That number gradually increased until we bumped up our giving to 50 percent about a decade ago.

How did we go from giving away 10 percent to giving away 50 percent? A simple way to understand the shift is to see that our money used to go into three buckets:

1. Operations (e.g., opening more stores)
2. Giving (at the beginning, 10 percent of profits)
3. Paying down our long-term debt

In the mid-1980s we started getting serious about paying off our debt, but only after long-term debt nearly sank us. As our debt shrank, we had more money to open more stores, which enabled us to give away even more. We also invested some of our profit.

Once we paid off our long-term debt, we said, "Wow, we don't have to pay down that debt any longer. Why don't we give away more of our profits?" After the long-term-debt bucket disappeared, we had more cash to put in the giving bucket. Around this time, I repeated a statement I'd made many times before: "You can't outgive God!" Immediately I had another of those divine episodes that always sparks some pivotal change.

Well, you've never really tried, have you? the Holy Spirit seemed to say to me. It felt like a direct challenge to back up my words. Not long afterward, we gave the largest amount we ever donated, and then began to add to that amount every six months. In time, we ended up giving away 50 percent of our annual profits.

Of course, no one can really outgive God, but merely saying the words is so easy and costs nothing. I believe God is pleased when we follow David's example. At a crucial point in Israel's history, the king was shown some plots of land on which the temple would be built. The man who owned the property offered to give his parcels to David, but the king replied, "No, but I will buy them for the full price. I will not take for the LORD what is yours, nor offer burnt offerings that cost me nothing" (1 Chron. 21:24 ESV).

We still have three buckets today, but we replaced the long-term-debt bucket with the investments bucket. When our investments do well, we can give away half of those earnings as well. We take our capital to make more capital so we can give away more. The better we do, in other words, the more money we can give away.

We're committed to giving away half of everything we make. That's what drives us. I don't know how much God may prompt you to give, but I do know that giving really is a crucial part of the secret sauce. I suppose it's something like salt: the sauce wouldn't be nearly the same without it.

Who Does It Help?

My eldest son, Mart, heads up our ministries investment committee. A report he created in late 2021 showed by category where and how much Hobby Lobby has given. Mart called it *25 Years of Giving.*

Over the past quarter of a century, we have given to 364 ministries. The top seven of them have received 80 percent of our funding, which reflects our philosophy of going deep with a few rather than shallow with many. The first year we gave, we funded only one ministry, a group that we still support today.

We almost never give to a new or failing ministry. We cannot, in good conscience, help groups or projects that haven't proved they work. We ask, "Why is God not blessing it?"

The Importance of Local Initiatives

Hobby Lobby calls Oklahoma City *home.* We live in the community, we have employees here, our headquarters are located here, people see us at local restaurants, they attend our church. Forty-four members of the Green family live in the Oklahoma City metropolitan area.

A PhD friend of Mart's recently stunned him when he said, "As you get closer and closer to the city where you live, your ministry gets larger and larger." It took some time for Mart to process that statement.

"I believe my friend was saying that we can be more incarnational in Oklahoma City than we can be someplace else, where we don't live," Mart said. "We can do ministry in other places and help there, but we're not incarnational there. People don't know us there. As we get closer to our own city, we have the potential to have more impact. We can live out our faith and be larger *here*. We still want to help the world, of course, and we do, but we also have this sense that our calling is growing larger in Oklahoma City."

Let me briefly outline a few of the local projects and initiatives we've undertaken. I'll start with an unusual one that took place more than two decades ago.

A Capitol Project

Although our ministry in and around Oklahoma City is growing, we have long felt the desire to help our community. Frank Keating, who served as Oklahoma's governor from 1995 to 2003, approached me one day to ask if we could help put a dome on our state capitol.

Construction on the capitol building finished in 1917, and while plans from 1914 had called for a dome, the state lacked the funds at the time to build one. World War I was just ending, then the Great Depression hit, then World War II erupted.

As one of the leading employers in this community, we agreed to help fund the building of the dome. The project wrapped up in 2002. While dome-building is not a typical project for us, and typically represents 1 percent or less of all our giving, we feel a responsibility to help with such initiatives whenever we can.

Flourish OKC

My grandson David Tyler works with Mart on our ministry investment team. Tyler feels passionate about the brokenness of our community, a passion that prompted him and his wife to move their young family into the inner city. His goal for the past few years has been to build trust with people in the inner city and to identify and work with their leaders. His biggest word is *relationships*. He has become friends with dozens of groups, discovering the amazing things they are already doing in our community. He longs for Oklahoma City to become a place "where all can flourish."

The work of Flourish OKC began through a hosted gala. In 2018, Bill High helped us to create an event in which various ministries throughout the city were honored and had the opportunity to share their work with the whole city. Each ministry honored received various amounts of funding through a traditional grant process.

While not all these groups focus on gospel ministry, as we do in most of our giving, they are all doing great work for marginalized individuals. We hope our small investment in them might point some individuals to Jesus when they hear, "These people are Christians, and look how they care for and value us."

When COVID hit, we realized there was a large amount of need that small ministries and nonprofits were facing in our city. Many of them would not qualify for relief funding and were facing great financial needs to access supplies and to continue regular and emergent operations. They needed safety items like masks, shields, and Plexiglas; and they all had unique needs to be met. Through asking the ministries and nonprofits "What do you need right now?," we were able to listen to what each group actually needed in that moment for their communities to thrive. We were also able to resource that need the best we could, whether that was through tangible items or funding. We gathered the major donors in our city and said to them, "All of these small ministries and nonprofits have needs, and many of them aren't sure how they will be able to make this work. Will you come together to fund this with us?"

Assisting Afghan Refugees

Through the Afghan Parolee Assistance Program, Oklahoma received eighteen hundred refugees from Afghanistan in 2021, more than any US state other than Texas or California. One thousand refugees were resettled in Oklahoma City and eight hundred in Tulsa.

Each year, Flourish OKC chooses a theme to provide focus for its activities. These themes are chosen through a process of listening and collaborating with city leaders and community members. Past years have focused on holistic education (2019) and restorative justice (2020). In 2021, Flourish OKC chose the theme "welcome"—months before any of us knew anything about the nearly two thousand Afghans about to arrive in Oklahoma. How's that for providential?

We had never received such a large group of refugees, and only two people in our community spoke their language. We therefore encouraged government leaders, ministry practitioners, and funders to get together on the phone once a week to strategize and ask, How can we help?

One early issue was transportation. We had five hundred Afghans staying in a single hotel, about three hundred of them children. Many families arrived with seven to nine kids; in the first sixty days after their arrival, seven babies were born. We had to get them all from the hotel to more permanent locations. How could we transport them there? We solved that critical issue together.

We want to serve the resettled refugee community well, whether that means helping them to successfully navigate a new culture (how do you drink out of a water fountain when you've never seen one?) or assisting them with housing, employment, or transportation. As Tyler often says, "We want to join together to walk toward a city where all flourish."

Prison Fellowship

Although we love prison ministry and have supported it through the years, until recently we hadn't done much with local prison ministries. So two years ago we approached Prison Fellowship and said, "Would you focus on Oklahoma City? What would it take for you to move to the next level here?"

As an outgrowth of Flourish OKC's 2020 theme of "restorative justice," we more than quadrupled our funding of Prison Fellowship. Since then, we have seen compassionate people from different vocations and backgrounds come together to serve prisoners, help them acclimate to life after prison, and also start projects to keep individuals from turning to crime. We have seen proof that lives can be restored and people do change. Tricia Everest, Oklahoma's secretary of public safety, said about the Hobby Lobby/Prison Fellowship partnership: "I can't think of anything better than paving the way for someone to find life where they have probably never found life in themselves before. . . . The seeds that are being planted? It's brilliant. I mean, these are beautiful trees of opportunity."

We count it a great joy to be part of Christ's work of love and renewal. It thrills us to see so many people working together to positively impact the entire penal system: those in prison, those coming out of prison, prison leaders, and the families of prisoners. All the wardens in our state now come together to receive training through Prison Fellowship's warden exchange program. They learn that God's Word does indeed make a difference! Current research proves that when you follow the Bible, your community has less crime.

How It Works

How do we invest our giving funds? We make those decisions by committee, a process we've used for about a quarter of a century. The seven-member ministry investment committee—made up of my wife, my three children, a son-in-law, a nephew, and me—meets once a month. All of us have worked together for at least forty years, including the five of us who started this business fifty years ago when our three kids were very young. Not until 1997 did the company start making enough profit that I felt we should collaboratively decide how and where to give.

We receive hundreds of funding requests each year, so to make things simple, I say, "Let's start by eliminating some of our options so we have fewer decisions to make." Too many decisions can harm our giving as much as they can harm our business. We typically give to about sixty groups each year.

Most often, we give to ministries that we know and already have helped. Most of our funded groups speak to some passion or relationship in the Green family. We're very passionate about God's Word, for example, as can be seen from our major support of the Museum of the Bible and Bible translation projects around the world.

As leader of the ministry investment team, Mart can decide, along with his team, how to spend perhaps 4 percent of our budget, which accounts for something like thirty of the organizations we fund each year. This practice allows our committee to focus on the much larger requests that make up about 95 percent of our total giving.

Before we meet, we all get a list of what we'll be voting on that day along with key data points for each ministry. Nothing comes to the committee unless it has a champion. We've all agreed to ask for God's help and guidance ahead of time, and we start each meeting with prayer. We then hear brief reports on each ministry and an explanation of how much they're requesting and how they intend to use the funds. Every ministry gets presented one at a time. We vote on each request before we proceed to the next one so that nobody gets confused.

We vote, silently, on separate Post-it notes so that none of us knows anyone else's vote. I don't want anybody to vote with me if their heart isn't in it. I want them to please God, not me. We love to get on board with organizations that God is clearly blessing because we want to see God roll out even more blessings.

I collect all votes and tally them. In general, we prefer that our gifts match the relative size of the organization receiving the gift. Suppose a ministry asks for $1 million but six of our seven committee members recommend $500,000 instead. We typically go with whatever number receives a majority of votes. But suppose four members vote for $500,000, two vote for $750,000, and one for $1 million. In that case, I may say, "Would everybody be willing to go to $750,000?" Often, they'll say yes, but sometimes, "No, can we vote again?"

While our process isn't super formal, it works. Our job is to be good stewards of God's money and to get a good return on our investment. The money belonged to Him before we earned it, and it's still His afterward.

What a thrill it is to see the Lord use these resources to bless people around the globe! I urge you to join us in both the work and the thrill.

Your Company Doesn't Have to Be Massive

One year while on a business trip to Hilton Head Island, Bill High met three brothers who run a custom-home building business. As they ate breakfast together, they told him about their business, which had seen good success over the years. Since Bill helps people give more, he asked them, "Okay, guys, how much are you giving?"

"We're giving 60 percent this year," they replied, "the maximum amount the government allows."

Bill could hardly believe it. *Sixty* percent? He asked them why. They said they had read *Giving It All Away . . . and Getting It All Back Again*[1] and felt inspired to give away as much as they could. These men give away *more* than half of their profit!

The principle of radical giving is not just for companies the size of Hobby Lobby. Though their business did well, these brothers made far less than most larger companies. Yet they still gave as much as they could, trusting God to take care of growing their business. The principle of radical giving is for everyone, including you.

Don't Let Fear Control You

I wonder if sometimes we avoid giving out of fear that we won't have enough left to grow our business or take care of our organization's needs. But God often leads in ways that don't seem to make much sense. Sometimes He leads us to give up our resources so that we don't depend on them more than we do on Him.

At Hobby Lobby we could have said, "God, we know You've called us into this business. We need to hold on to these profits so we can grow." But we saw *greater* growth after we started giving more. I believe God sometimes pares down our resources so that when we see success, we know it did not come from us.

Is God calling you to give more than you feel comfortable giving? Don't limit God. Don't insist that you need to hold on to profits to accomplish your goals. When you invest in the eternal and give God control of your resources, He can do more with less. This, too, is part of the secret sauce.

What's More Important than Profit?

When we closed our stores on Sundays many years ago, we believed it was the right thing to do, even though Sundays were our most profitable day. Although our sales increased shortly after we made that decision, we didn't know what would happen when we acted. We simply chose to follow God's lead even though we thought it would reduce our profit.

Obedience to God may cost you, but some things are more important than profit.

Barbara and I always tithed our personal earnings. Early on, we also gave corporately through Hobby Lobby. But once we committed to giving some scary amounts—amounts beyond what we thought we could afford—that's when the company really started taking off.

God has blessed Hobby Lobby immensely, which we know is tied to our giving. Still, the Bible does not promise us more business success if we give more. At Hobby Lobby, we don't give more so we can get more; we get more so we can give more. We have come to experience the truth of Acts 20:35: "It is more blessed to give than to receive."

We figure that if we give away one more dollar, we will have that much more joy. That's why we make as much profit as we can so that we can give away as much as we can.

They Know It Works

I know of a business owner, a shrimper, whose business suffered tremendously when a hurricane severely damaged his boats. All his boats needed extensive repairs, and he didn't see how he could afford to follow through on the monetary commitment he had made to a ministry focused on helping children around the world. He gave anyway—and the following year, his business had the best shrimp harvest it had ever seen. God more than repaid this shrimper for his gift.

Pete Ochs, owner of Seat King and other businesses, has seen his own miracles from giving. He began his career in the commercial investment business, then started his own investment banking company at age thirty. Ten years later, he began buying his own portfolio of companies.

Around this time, Pete and his wife, Deb, tried to help a ministry's fundraising campaign. Deb felt a push from the

Lord that she and Pete needed to sell their most profitable company in the portfolio, a healthcare company, and give the profits to the ministry to fully fund it.

"Are you *crazy?*" Pete asked his wife. "That company is our goose that lays the golden egg! Look how much money we've been able to give away from owning it."

"I just feel like we need to sell it," she insisted.

They debated the issue over the weekend and finally agreed that the Lord wanted them to sell the company. On Monday, Pete called two corporations he knew would have an interest in buying. "Send us your offers by Friday," he said, "because we're ready to sell."

Both companies offered his full asking price. One offered stock, while the other offered cash. Pete and Deb chose the company with the cash offer since they wanted to gift it right away to the ministry. They gave sacrificially, and the ministry met its fundraising goals.

Two weeks after Pete signed the sales agreement, Congress passed a law reducing Medicare reimbursement rates by 40 percent. About 90 percent of the revenue of Pete's old company came from Medicare. Once the new law went into effect, the company's revenue plummeted, and within two years the parent company went out of business.

Pete thought he was giving sacrificially when he sold the company, but God's leading protected this couple from significant financial loss.

Pete credits his willingness to give with a tolerance for risk. "So many times, we want to hold on tightly when we think it's ours," he said. "But if we see ourselves as stewards, risk isn't a Las-Vegas-style roll of the dice. Risk is a prayed-up, planned-up, prepared-up approach to life. It's really just figuring out what God wants you to do and then doing it."

Listen to God's leading. If God tells you to give, then give. You might not know why. It might not make sense at the time. Give anyway. God sees the whole picture, and He has incredible things in mind that we can't even begin to imagine.

FOUR

MAXIMIZE RISK FOR THE RIGHT REASONS

What makes a company great? Many of those asking the question point to the book *Good to Great: Why Some Companies Make the Leap and Others Don't*. While I'm sure that book offers a great deal of helpful advice, it measures success primarily by longevity of stock value. The higher a company's stock prices soar and the longer they stay there, the greater the company.

But is high stock price really the chief measure of success? I say the publisher mistitled the book. It might more accurately be titled, *Good to Better*.

In my view, no company can become truly great unless it focuses on eternity. Without that, we just tweak a few little things here and there without ever achieving true greatness.

The Real Bottom Line

When God told me, *I've put these employees in your charge* (see chapter 7), I knew that a big part of obeying His call required caring deeply for their souls. That's our real bottom line.

But what does it mean to care for souls? The concept of souls as the real bottom line strays far outside of the box for most businesses.

The Bible says, "The grass withers and the flowers fall, but the word of our God endures forever" (Isa. 40:8). God's Word lasts forever. Does anything else? Yes! Jesus says, "The one who believes in me will live, even though they die; and whoever lives by believing in me will never die" (John 11:25–26). Human souls last forever too. So if God's Word and people's souls both last forever, then shouldn't they be the bottom line for success as a company?

Only what you do for God will last for eternity. Everything else disappears: money disappears, fame disappears, promotions disappear. Only two things are eternal: God's Word and human souls.

No matter what other service you might perform, souls are your true bottom line. What does this mean for your specific situation? No blanket rule exists for how to care for souls. But simply put, bring God's Word into your work, prioritize people, and then listen for the Holy Spirit's guidance.

Two Lives

Have you ever driven through a dense fog? In the cool hours of the morning, you see nothing but the fog. The road seems to disappear, cars vanish, and the fields cloak themselves in a thick mantle of gray. The fog seems never-ending. But even the thickest fog always disappears an hour or so after the sun comes out.

Our lives are like that fog. We have two distinct lives, our vapor life and our eternal life. The Bible says, "You are a mist that appears for a little while and then vanishes" (James 4:14). We're here for a short time, and then we're gone. When our vapor life ends, eternal life begins in earnest.

In a dense fog we see nothing but fog, but it merely obscures reality. It sticks around only until the sun burns it away. In a similar way, this earthly life can feel like the only thing that exists. We see nothing else. But it, too, will quickly disappear, just like a vapor. Only our second life will remain, our eternal life.

What activities consume your attention right now that won't matter in a hundred years? As a leader, can you afford such a short-term focus?

We live in an era when most Americans know nothing about eternity. They don't know that Jesus died for our sins, was buried, and on the third day rose from the dead to forgive their sins. They have no idea that the instant they put their faith in Christ, they receive eternal life. We live in tragic times.

So if we're Christians, how can we obsess on expanding our profits? That makes no sense to me. If we have two lives, a vapor one and an eternal one, shouldn't we focus most of our energy on the eternal one?

If I have two investment portfolios, one that disappears after ten years and one that lasts for a thousand years, which should I emphasize? Clearly, the longer lasting one. How foolish to invest all my money in the short-term one! At Hobby Lobby, we want to put as much of our profits as possible toward eternity.

What's your focus? Do you spend most of your energy on this vapor life or on the life to come? Hobby Lobby gives away half of its profits every year because we believe that true success is sharing the good news of Jesus Christ with as many as we can. The more profitable we grow, the more ministries we can fund and the more lives we can impact for eternity. That, I believe, is the only way to become truly great.

The Joy of Sharing

When we compare the emptiness of stuff with the joy of knowing one more person will be in heaven because of a gift we gave, there's no comparison. We get great joy from telling people about Christ. For us, it's just plain fun.

Most of our giving at Hobby Lobby goes to gospel-focused ministries and to projects that center on salvation and the gift of God's Word. Maybe an organization you support drills wells to provide clean water to impoverished communities. That's good! But wouldn't it be even better to drill wells *and* provide the life-giving message about the God who loves us? Jesus asks, "What does it profit a man to gain the whole world and forfeit his soul?" (Mark 8:36 ESV). Yes, let's provide services for the body, but let's also provide the message of eternal life in Jesus Christ.

For more than two decades, we have strongly supported the ministry of OneHope. God has allowed us, through OneHope, to present the gospel to more than a billion kids. A *billion*. Through Every Home for Christ, another Christian ministry we have long supported, we have reached a billion homes with the gospel message.

Which would you rather have? Another house? A boat? A fleet of cars? Or another person in heaven because of a gift you gave? A billion dollars or a billion people in heaven? Hands down, this is a no-brainer for us. Why live for the vapor life when you can live for the eternal one?

We periodically invite representatives from the ministries we support to come to our headquarters to describe their work. Life.Church, for example, has shown us what it accomplishes through its popular Bible app, YouVersion.

Samaritan's Purse is a ministry that runs Operation Christmas Child, a program in which donors pack shoeboxes with toys to be sent overseas to children in need. Because we sell the shoeboxes in our stores to promote the ministry, Samaritan's Purse sent us a representative to describe its work. She told us how, as a young girl in the Middle East, she received one of these shoeboxes that contained a small transistor radio. She listened to it for hours. That gift changed her life, connecting her to a bigger world and reminding her that somebody on the other side of the globe cared about her. As a Christian, she viewed the shoebox as an answer to her prayers. In the middle of persecution and poverty, the shoebox reminded her God saw her and loved her. When she grew up, she moved to the United States. She now works for Samaritan's Purse in Boone, North Carolina, so that she can offer kids the same gift of love that she received so many years before.

Our employees tell us that working for Hobby Lobby is unique because they know their work has eternal impact. While we can each separately tithe our incomes and make little gifts here and there, as a company we've chosen to give away hundreds of millions of dollars to ministries and projects designed to connect people with God.

Hobby Lobby employees get to see firsthand how they are an important part of something *much* bigger than themselves. Many feel far more motivated than if their work went only toward lining the pockets of shareholders. They know their work has eternal impact. Every extra dollar they can save or earn Hobby Lobby is another dollar going toward eternity.

Risking for Souls

If souls really are the true bottom line, then Christian leaders must be willing to minimize their monetary profit to grow their true bottom line for eternity.

Hobby Lobby has a strong focus on monetary profit, of course, as all successful businesses must. In fact, Hobby Lobby is the most profitable retail chain per dollar in the country. Another retailer would have to spend two to three dollars to make the same amount of profit we do by spending just one dollar.

By *minimizing profit* I mean that we don't stop at being merely the most financially profitable. We want to make as much money as we can, as long as we can, to tell as many people about Christ as we can. We invest in eternity, the best investment possible—and investing always entails risk.

Like any company, Hobby Lobby has money tied up in financial investments, each of which carries a certain risk. We try to balance low- and high-risk investments, but all involve some risk.

Now, what kind of leader would I be if I were willing to put money at risk to earn more money but refused to risk for people's souls? That just doesn't seem right.

"I am not ashamed of the gospel," Paul declares, "because it is the power of God that brings salvation to everyone who believes" (Rom. 1:16). As a Christian, I believe in the gospel, the good news that Jesus came to earth to make it possible for all of us to live forever with Him in heaven. This is every person's only hope for a blessed eternity—and as the senior leader at Hobby Lobby, I am honest about it. Sure, it might be risky to be so open about my faith, but I believe it is well worth the investment. What, after all, is the worth of one human soul?

The first time we included an opportunity for employees to respond to a gospel invitation at a comanager meeting, our general counsel asked to speak with me afterward. Peter felt concerned that someone might object to our bringing up faith in the workplace and that a lawsuit could cost us a great deal of money.

"Fifteen people gave their lives to Christ today," I replied. "You tell me—what is the cost of a soul?"

Peter teared up and silently walked out of my office. And for as long as we have offered gospel invitations, no one has complained about us sharing our family's faith with them or giving them an opportunity to respond to the gospel.

Still, the risk remains. Hobby Lobby stands for some things that make us a target. When we send out our Fourth of July ad or our Easter ad, for example—both of them evangelistic appeals and not sales advertisements—we see denial-of-service attacks on our website. We prepare for those attacks just before and after they happen. We invest in tools designed to stay one step ahead of the assaults. So then, are our stands for life and for Jesus worth it? I stand with Paul: "I consider that our present sufferings are not worth comparing with the glory that will be revealed in us" (Rom. 8:18).

Leaders can accomplish great things when they take seriously the care of human souls. We must never be pushy or pressure anyone. But we can give opportunities. We can be open about what we believe and give our colleagues the opportunity to do the same.

As a leader, how are you creating opportunities for those around you to know God? If your organization's effectiveness were to be evaluated by how it cared for people's souls, how would it rank? Have you settled in your heart that the risk is worth the payoff?

Life from Death

A Hobby Lobby store employee once had a heart attack and passed away in a back office of the store. His associate, an employee we'll call Maria, was with him at the time. Maria and her colleagues had to wait with the body until an emergency medical worker came, declared the man dead, and removed the corpse. The incident traumatized Maria.

As soon as Debbie Kinsey, our director of management ministries, heard about the incident, she headed to that store. She sat in the manager's office, making herself available to any associate who wanted help in processing the shock and grief.

When Maria walked in, Debbie realized that in her hurry to get to the store, she had left her Bible in a rental car. As she spoke with a shaken Maria, Debbie could not remember a single Scripture verse. Although she had been in ministry for years, her mind went blank. She could think only of John 3:16, so she personalized it for Maria: "For God so loved you, Maria . . ."

Before she could finish the verse, Maria burst into tears. When she could talk again, she told Debbie, "After I saw him die, I realized I had no assurance I was going to heaven, if it was my time. And I just needed to know there was still hope. I prayed, 'God, I just need to know that you still love me.'"

Debbie then shared the entire verse with her: "For God so loved the world that he gave his one and only Son, that whoever believes in him shall not perish but have eternal life." Maria gave her heart to the Lord right there in the office. She returned home, called her estranged mother, and led her to Christ too. Over time, other family members also put their faith in Jesus.

Debbie has many such stories. One of my favorites began at a comanager meeting where Debbie gave out a hodgepodge of leftover trinkets, including a cheap little compass. She almost didn't put the compass in the bag, it was so cheap. But since she didn't want to waste it, she threw it in.

She held the meeting, then later that week traveled to a new store's grand opening. After the ceremony, a comanager who had attended the earlier meeting walked up to Debbie, tears in his eyes.

"Do you have a minute?" he asked. When they stepped to the side, away from the crowd, he told her his story.

"When I was in the comanager meeting earlier this week and heard you speak, I got this compass. I looked around, and while everybody else got nice little gifts, I got the cheapest little thing."

He told Debbie he had been feeling down on his luck, as though the whole world were against him. *Great*, he thought, *even here I get the short end of the stick*. He threw the compass in his coat pocket and thought no more about it. He returned to his home city.

At work the next day, as he walked across the parking lot to his store, he reached in his pocket and felt the compass.

"You can believe it or not," he told Debbie, "but God spoke to me there in the parking lot. He said, '*You are going the wrong direction and I'm here to tell you that you need to have Me in your life. I will give you direction.*' I gave my heart to God right there before I even walked in the store. The item I had thought was the cheapest little thing, the one that made me question 'Why me?' turned out to be the very thing that turned my life around."

As a leader, how are you planting seeds for the gospel? You may not see results for a long time, but they will come. God promises that just as rain falls from clouds and doesn't return until it has accomplished its purpose of watering the earth, so God's Word always accomplishes its purpose (Isa. 55:10–11). It is worth the extra effort to be creative in caring for souls, even if results come only later.

We might consider such soul care the protein in our secret sauce. That's the ingredient that makes people strong and healthy.

Yes, She Can Do That

Debbie Kinsey is really an evangelist. She attends grand openings of new Hobby Lobby stores. She typically opens these events with prayer. We have several reports of city and state officials coming to these events who hear her and say, "You can do that?"

Yes, she can do that.

Some of those officials have responded, "Oh, I'm going to start that too."

Debbie attends every time we host our comanagers for an orientation meeting. She speaks on the first morning of these meetings and prays "the sinner's prayer" with whoever wants to join her. Those who respond can fill out cards that say, "I accepted Christ for the first time" or "I rededicated my life to Jesus." She tells me that of the sixty comanagers who attend a typical meeting, about 80 percent say they accepted Christ for the first time or rededicated their life to the Lord.

One time during a manager meeting, Debbie noticed one of the comanagers sitting by herself in the conference room and discovered that because of her religious background, she could not enjoy the lunch prepared.

Debbie apologized, offered to go get her different food, and showed her love. We learned later that this new employee had never experienced a genuine, caring kind of love and concern. By the end of the meeting, she came to Debbie and said, "I want you to know that I accepted Christ."

I often hear reports like these or get letters from those whose lives have changed in some way because of their connection to Hobby Lobby. Very often they say it's because they have carefully observed some of our leaders follow hard after Christ.

What leaders in your organization follow so hard after Christ that others want to become more like Jesus too? Is this part of your own secret sauce?

Prayer at the Checkout Line

Sometimes obedience doesn't cost us in dollars or profit, but it can cost in other ways.

One of our assistant managers kept noticing a woman in the checkout line. The assistant manager sensed that God wanted her to pray for the lady, but she felt hesitant to walk up to a stranger with such an out-of-the-blue request. Still, she couldn't shake the feeling.

When the woman finished checking out, the assistant manager approached her gently and said, "Would it be possible for me to have a word of prayer with you?"

The woman started crying. "I can't believe you're doing this," she said.

It turned out the woman desperately needed prayer. Through tears, she described her difficult situation, and the assistant manager prayed for her. Throughout the interchange, both the nearby cashier and the customers standing in line stopped to watch. When she finished praying, the cashier also prayed. And then the customers prayed for the lady too, right where they stood in l ine!

This interaction cost us no money but still carried a degree of risk. How would the customer respond to the assistant manager's unexpected question? How would observers react? What if she prayed and her words came out all wrong?

While obedience often carries risk, listening to the Holy Spirit's prompting always pays off. In this encounter, both the assistant manager and her tearful customer walked away with a stronger faith.

The Pull of Purpose

What makes Hobby Lobby different? Not long ago our head of IT, Jeanne Cotter, surveyed her 250 employees on a WebEx, asking them, "What do you think is different about this place?" They emailed her their answers, and when she aggregated them all, she discovered that the word *purpose* came up far more than any other.

That word, of course, can mean different things to various people. But whether respondents tied it to the many outreaches supported by Hobby Lobby or to their personal sense of purpose in their jobs, purpose resoundingly came out number one.

One of our young developers wrote an application to schedule trash pickups at stores. In its first year of use, the app saved the company a million dollars. When the IT department celebrated the success of the trash app, the young developer thought, *I made that!*

"At the end of the day," Jeanne said, "we connected the dots from that app to making a big difference in the company. Purpose ties all the way through. We help our people understand that it's not just about profitability but what Hobby Lobby is doing with those profits. What really makes this place special is that we're working for something bigger than ourselves."

Are you working for something bigger than yourself? More specifically, are you working for the biggest thing of all, caring for human souls? Yes, this work carries risk, but it also promises a deep and lasting thrill—an eternal one. I invite you to join other energized leaders who find their core purpose in partnering with God Himself on the greatest adventure in the universe.

PART TWO

PEOPLE-CENTERED PRACTICES

Five

BUILD FOR 150 YEARS, NOT JUST THE NEXT GENERATION

If you had the opportunity to peer 150 years into the future to check on the health and well-being of your descendants and your organization, would you do it?

Some would jump at the invitation, expecting to find vibrant fifth- or sixth-generation family members thriving and enjoying life, playing a vital role in society, and remaining deeply committed to the values and faith of their forebears.

Others would flatly refuse, choosing instead to see only in their imaginations a wonderful vision full of happiness and joy. Why risk glimpsing a much gloomier picture filled with pain, regret, and suffering?

Still others, I suspect, would hesitate. And probably for a long, long time.

What would *you* choose? And why?

I doubt any of us will ever get such a sneak peek into the future, but what if we could stack the odds in our favor? What if we could begin to create a positive rather than a putrid future for our descendants and the organizations we've worked so hard to build? What if we could do a few key things *now* to affect better life outcomes *later*? While I can't build us a time machine, I can suggest some time-tested ideas that, though not typical, can set up both you and your future heritage for success *and* significance.

Business Prospects and Family Future

In the early stages of a startup organization, leaders spend most of their time focusing on survival with little thought for long-term planning. Worries about how to survive to the end of the year don't typically spark musings about next-generation leadership.

If the organization survives—and most don't—it transitions eventually from interdependence (all hands on deck!) to independence. Leaders relax a bit. The founders may even go on to do other things. The focus of leadership moves from survival to expansion.

At some point, those who sacrificed to help the organization succeed often look back and say, "It took a lot of time, energy, and effort to grow this business. It took pain—and I don't want my family to suffer the same pain I did." So they try to shelter their kids and their descendants from that pain. They want those who come after them to continue reaping the benefits of their hard work and sacrifices. They typically do this by handing down stock to their children so their kids can expect a comfortable income for years to come. Financial advisors tell them to "minimize taxes, hand out shares to your children." Estate planners say the same thing.

Suggestions like these can sound good on the surface. Why not give kids ownership and let them run the business after the founders retire or die? Usually, however, that's as far as our "long-term" planning goes, to one generation and perhaps to the next—nothing beyond that.

I'd call such a practice both shortsighted and dangerously short-term. It's dangerous to focus on only the next generation. Both your business/organization and your children/descendants deserve better than that.

The question is, What strategies can you use *today* to lay the foundation for a better future *tomorrow*? Let's consider business issues and family concerns separately, even though they're intimately connected. I'd like to start with business, the topic I consider the less important of the two but nevertheless an issue of great significance.

Businesses that Last

Anyone who knows me can tell you that I'm not much for reading the *Harvard Business Review*. The title of this book, *Leadership Not by the Book*, should tell you that the way we operate at Hobby Lobby runs contrary to most contemporary business advice. We don't do things the way students learn to do business at Harvard Business School.

Still, the title of an *HBR* article from a few years ago, "How Winning Organizations Last 100 Years," sounded interesting. Who wouldn't like to know what century-old businesses might be doing in common? One hundred years isn't 150 years, of course, but it's moving in the right direction.

The authors studied seven successful organizations, each one with at least a century of history. The organizations ranged from the New Zealand All Blacks rugby team to the Royal Shakespeare Company. Researchers spent five years observing these groups (which they called "Centennials"), interviewing employees and former employees, observing their day-to-day operations, and reading extensively about them. "Surprisingly," they wrote, "we found the Centennials are all very similar to each other, despite their different vocations—and behave in ways that defy conventional wisdom."[1]

Hobby Lobby has earned a reputation for behaving "in ways that defy conventional wisdom," so I thought it might be interesting to hear what the authors had to say.

The article continued, "Most businesses focus on serving customers, owning resources, being efficient and growing—but the Centennials don't. Instead, they try to shape society, share experts, create accidents, and focus on getting better not bigger. They're radically traditional—with a stable core, but a disruptive edge. And that's what keeps them ahead."[2]

I consider Hobby Lobby also to be "radically traditional" with a "stable core." While this article didn't convince me to read more Harvard publications, it did have some intriguing insights.

The article identifies three primary elements about both the core and the disruptive edge of each of the Centennials. Not all of them fit Hobby Lobby, but many do. First, the core:

- *Stable purpose.* The Centennials "are incredibly strategic, looking 20 to 30 years ahead, to understand how society is evolving, how they can shape it, and how they can get the talent to do this."[3]

- *Stable stewardship.* While most organizations change leadership every five years, the Centennials "keep [leaders] in place for more than 10. Not just at the top of the organization, but two or three levels further down too—where key knowledge and influence often sits. And they carefully manage leadership transitions, so nothing is lost along the way."[4] The Centennials look for leaders who are "humble stewards, who are keen to learn from the previous leader, and who are more concerned about the organization they'll leave behind than how it looks while they're there."[5]

- *Stable openness.* The Centennials all "perform in public" to "raise the organization's profile."

They "deliberately open themselves up to invite scrutiny and create pressure" and also "find great things to do and then share them with the world through books, articles and films."[6]

I hope you recognize in these comments many of the elements of a successful enterprise that I'm recommending throughout this book. A business that wants to thrive must have a stable core, know who and what it is, and remain true to its purpose and personality. A stable core, however, is not enough. Success also calls for a disruptive edge, which according to these researchers also has three primary elements:

- *Disruptive experts.* In an effort to "stay fresh and create a continuous flow of new ideas," the Centennials "go out looking for new ideas—but not by tracking the competition. . . . Instead, they work out who's the best in the world at something and try to learn from them." They also recruit from outside their sector "to bring in new knowledge and experience."[7] They insist on staying creative, dynamic, and on the lookout for better ways to do their work.

- *Disruptive nervousness.* Both success and growth make the Centennials nervous. A representative of the Royal College of Art said, "We need to be big enough to create impact and be financially stable, but not so big that we get distracted or lose control." They take care to make sure their standards don't slip, they obsess over details, and they "prefer to make lots of tiny tweaks, rather than looking for large breakthroughs."[8]

• *Disruptive accidents.* The Centennials want their people to mingle and work on different projects "to create movement and bumps." Employees from various disciplines "continually question each other, and share problems, ideas, and opportunities."

I appreciate how these Centennials maintain their purpose while branching out into unknown territory: "While stabilizing their core, the Centennials keep waves of disruption crashing at their edge—to stay fresh and get better."[9]

While we all need to stay fresh and get better, the question is, Will these practices and strategies help an organization stay vibrant and true to its core for 150 years? Since I can't see into the future, I can't say for sure. But if they've worked for a century, they probably will work for at least another fifty years. Certainly, most businesses could benefit from at least exploring them. Did you know that the average life span of an S&P 500 company has plunged by 80 percent in the last eighty years? The typical business life of these companies has declined from sixty-seven years to just fifteen.[10]

The key question for me, however, is not *how* to set up a business to last 150 years but *why* it should matter if it endures that long. Why would you want your business or organization to last another century and a half? What is it accomplishing right now? Why would you want to perpetuate whatever it's doing now?

Hobby Lobby doesn't exist merely to sell arts and crafts. Selling merchandise is essentially a means to an end. I've always had several purposes in mind for our company, including to provide for my family; to offer a decent living to my employees; to bless the community where we live and work; to introduce men, women, and children to the salvation found only in Jesus; to advance God's kingdom worldwide; and to glorify the Lord. I want Hobby Lobby to endure *long* past my lifetime so that the company can continue to pursue all these things.

But allow me to ask, Why do you want *your* business or organization to endure?

Inheritance or Heritage?

Do you want to leave your children and descendants an inheritance or a heritage? There's a big difference between the two.

An inheritance refers to the material resources you bequeath to your children and heirs upon your death. A heritage refers more to the spiritual riches and deep-seated treasures of character that wise parents leave to their children.

An inheritance most often includes things such as money, real estate, property, stocks and bonds, and ownership of companies and businesses. Stocks and company ownership often get passed on to heirs through trusts and similar legal structures that supposedly reflect long-term thinking. But too often, such thinking focuses on only a single generation, maybe two at best. Parents might therefore set up legal structures such as generation-skipping trusts, but they still keep handing down stock and ownership from one generation to the next. And that can cause significant problems.

Consider my own family. Barbara and I are first generation (Gen 1). But we have three adult children, all married; they're Gen 2. If we wanted to pass down dividend-bearing stock from Hobby Lobby, six people would inherit ownership stock. For simplicity's sake, let's suppose that all ten grandchildren marry; that would mean twenty people splitting ownership at the Gen 3 level. Supposing that each grandchild has three kids and each kid marries, we would have sixty people in Gen 4.

The question then becomes, Is the business big enough to support sixty shareholders? Perhaps so, but what about the possible 180 people in the subsequent generation?

More than likely, at least half of these shareholders won't even work in the business, but they'll still show up at board meetings as voting members. What happens if 60 percent of these shareholders one day say to a new CEO, "We don't like you, and we want our money"? They can vote to sell the company and take the cash. I've seen this happen. I've watched the original, good work of founders go up in smoke.

A failure to think long-term can also destroy an organization's culture. The founder sacrifices much to grow the business and build a culture that reflects a certain set of values. At Hobby Lobby, I've tried to build a company that serves people and honors the Lord. If we passed along ownership of Hobby Lobby to shareholders who had never worked there, how could they keep the culture? They couldn't.

What, then, would happen to our staff? We have fifty thousand employees. If we didn't plan for long-term leadership continuity, our lack of foresight would likely one day trigger a forced sale and a vanishing corporate culture. All Hobby Lobby families would suffer. We simply can't let that happen. That's why I'm far more concerned about leaving a good heritage than a big inheritance.

The Benefits of 150-Year Planning

Organizations that plan for the long term typically last for the long term. Consider the financial business created by the Rothschild family.

Mayer Amschel Rothschild lived in Frankfurt, Germany, in the eighteenth century, where he established a banking business. He trained each of his sons to open a branch in another European country. Hundreds of years later, his descendants still work in banking and investments.[11]

Or think of the Japanese brand Kikkoman, commonly known for its soy sauce. In the 1600s, the Mogi family started brewing and selling soy sauce. In 1917, their descendants joined with two other Japanese families who continued passing company ownership down through the family. A family member still presides as CEO and chairman.[12] The firm's leadership structure has allowed it to preserve its culture and values, which in turn have preserved the business.[13]

In both examples, the companies have spanned hundreds of years, continuing to grow and adapt to a changing world without losing their core identities. They created cultures that have lasted for centuries. In doing so, their businesses have continued to serve millions of people.

But how? How did they achieve such long-term sustainability?

How to Succeed Long-Term

Companies and organizations don't last forever by default. For both, long-term success takes careful planning.

Bill High has made 150-year planning a strong focus of his ministry, Vyne Legacy. Bill helped my own family set up our mission, vision, and values, which have become part of our governance structure, preparing us for corporate succession. He also leads two-day workshops to help families think and plan generationally, helping them pass on not just finances but faith. Those workshops contain many of the principles you'll read here. We've worked hard to figure out ways to protect the ministry of Hobby Lobby for many decades to come. I hope the lessons we've learned may also help you.

Choose Interdependence Based on Values

Organizations start out interdependent—they need others to stay alive. As they succeed, they reach a point of independence. They can sit back and say, "We're good." Precisely at this point, many organizations start to decline. Leaders can begin to entitle or enrich themselves, taking their eyes off the ball and delegating so much that they have little to do. They get distracted and look for other activities to fill their time. They buy a plane or a boat; they begin an affair. Not needing to work produces all kinds of problems.

Many top-level CEOs who reach this place insulate themselves. They become independent, thinking they need no one, including God. That's when the organization starts to really plummet.

How can leaders avoid this decline? When they reach independence, they must choose to stay dependent. This time around, however, they must choose a dependence based on values, not on financial need.

The secret sauce here encourages you to keep all hands on deck, not because you have no other choice but because you all have a common goal and hold common values. You all are part of a bigger cause. By choosing to remain interdependent, you can sustain an organization long past the departure of its founder.

Unite around a Cause, Not a Personality

Most organizations begin by building around a personality, as when a hard-driving entrepreneur creates

96

something out of nothing. If you want to make your business last, however, you must move from a dynamic personality to a dynamic cause.

Voice of the Martyrs has lasted for sixty years. Richard and Sabina Wurmbrand founded VOM in 1967 after escaping imprisonment in communist Romania. When Christians in Norway convinced their government to "buy" Richard from Romania (they had started selling political prisoners for money), Wurmbrand's story spread quickly. News outlets in the United States, Europe, and Asia all carried his story and thus began his ministry of traveling the globe and opening more than thirty offices to care for persecuted Christians around the world.[14] VOM has continued to grow after Wurmbrand's death in 2001, successfully making the leadership transition by uniting volunteers and staff around a clear cause—serving the persecuted church. Shared values have enabled the ministry to expand beyond its gifted founder.

Set Up Structures for Continuity

Create a structure that allows the organization to govern itself regardless of who's in charge. Think long-term, which implies governance, structure, and constitution. What can you set up now that will continue long after you're gone?

The founders of our nation did this. They carefully set up a system of government that has lasted nearly 250 years. They foresaw the danger of autocrats trying to rule and created a system of checks and balances to prevent it.

The executive, legislative, and judicial branches each have their own areas of authority, a system designed to thwart individuals attempting to take over the country.

Hobby Lobby did a similar thing when it set up its current structure. As already noted, we have separate committees for giving, investments, stewardship, and governance. No single individual holds all the power. This structure keeps us dependent on one another and is designed to keep Hobby Lobby from splintering as one generation follows another.

Building a long-term legacy is not the same as giving a fortune to your kids. Long-term planning means creating a structure that perpetuates values from one generation to the next. Finances play just one part in successful long-term planning.

Provide Clear Criteria for Future Leaders (Trustees, Board Members, Etc.)

Without specifying clear criteria that spell out the qualifications for corporate leadership, no organization can succeed for 150 years. Having the right person in charge is far more important than some leader carrying the family's DNA.

Personality is God-given. Some people have leadership gifts and others don't. Naming someone the leader of an organization just because they have the founder's genes makes no more sense than choosing a donkey to fly a plane because it has the same color as the airline's logo. Maybe the role of CEO requires an extroverted visionary, but a potential Gen 2 or Gen 3 candidate lacks the right disposition or gifting. It's best not to force it.

Just as important, no organization can afford to overlook character. A good leader must have both the appropriate gifting and the necessary character. If a family member has those things, great! But having the right person in place is far more important than having someone with the "right" DNA.

At Hobby Lobby, we have a set of criteria that any individual must meet before becoming a board member or trustee. This list remains the same regardless of whether the person carries the last name Green. Criteria trumps family. Every company must continue to have capable leaders in place, or it will crumble. For us, the ministry that Hobby Lobby makes possible is too important to let the company collapse.

Continue Being Creative in Every Generation of Leadership

Companies decline when they stop being creative. While an early, hard-driving, creative personality often gets an organization going, too many subsequent generations try to live off of the founder's creativity. It never works. Decline begins the moment a generation of leaders chooses to ride on the coattails of a past generation's accomplishments. An organization can thrive only so long as each generation continues to mine its own creativity, using it to continually improve the organization. Continued success requires continued creativity.

We are all creative because all of us are made in the image of God, our Creator. God challenged the very first human being to name all the animals that He had created—and Adam pulled it off. It was a stupendous act of creativity! The same kind of creativity that flowed through Adam's veins flows through ours.

Creativity is not only for artists or performers. Businesspeople and organizational leaders must learn how to tap the creativity God placed inside them to tackle and overcome every challenge they face. Trying to lean on a founder's creativity is like trying to read by last year's sunlight.

Plan Now for the Long Haul

If you don't think long-term for your organization, future generations will pay the price for your negligence. Long-term planning means far more than just thinking of you and your kids or your next generation of leadership. It means planning for the next 150 years.

What if you really did have a time machine that enabled you to glimpse your family's future one and a half centuries from now? What would you hope to see?

Many businesses have a defined set of vision, mission, and value statements that guide their company. Why don't we do the same for our families?

I encourage you to play out this little scenario. Set aside some time to sit down, close your eyes, and imagine the lives of your great-great-great-great-grandchildren. What would you like to see pictured on the pulsating screen of your time machine? Once you have a clear idea, open your eyes and write down what you "saw." Also write down what you *don't* want to see. Get as specific as possible. Based on what you hope to see, write down a 150-year generational vision. Make the vision statement as exciting and captivating as possible—something that will inspire future generations.

Once you've written down your vision, now comes the hard part! What must you start doing *now* to make it more likely that your vision comes true *then*? This part of the exercise will take longer than a few minutes. But if you entertain any hope of having an outsized impact on your world through the work of your organization, business, or enterprise, you must give long and careful thought to this ingredient of the secret sauce. I'm confident it will pay huge dividends. But producing those dividends will require your commitment to doing the work *now*. Nothing less will suffice.

DRIVE FAMILY PRACTICES, NOT PROFIT PRACTICES

I once threw a business book in the trash. Do you want to know why?

A Christian author had written about how to succeed in business, and I wanted to hear what he had to say. His advice seemed fairly helpful—until I got about halfway through the book. Then he suggested that career success meant no one should allow their marriage to get in the way of building a thriving business.

That was enough for me. The author could not have gotten it more wrong. I stopped reading and threw away the book.

Family First . . . *Really?*

Most of us probably would agree with the saying "Family first." But as leaders, we often subconsciously add the word *after*, as in, I'll put my family first

> *after* the business stabilizes.
> *after* I'm done working on my master's degree.
> *after* I complete my PhD.
> *after* I finish this work project.
> *after* we run this new fundraising campaign.

We adopt this attitude without realizing there will *always* be a next thing. We say "family first," but too often we don't live it out. Maybe we get caught up in ambition, or we give lip service to the concept, but our actions reveal that we think we can do it all on our own. I have seen too many leaders stretch themselves so thin that they neglect the most important aspects of life.

If you postpone the important things until some less busy day, you will wait forever. That day will never come. You will never believe you have enough time. It takes faith to prioritize people right now when doing so might risk losing sales or falling behind in your career.

Inc. magazine interviewed entrepreneurs to discover their biggest regrets. Their number one lament was "not spending enough time with friends and family." Respondents regretted the many hours they poured into the business at the expense of their most important relationships.[1]

As leaders, we have to consider whether we are inadvertently sending the wrong message—"Work hard now so you can spend time with your family later." Particularly in the early stage of organizations, we easily excuse long hours for both ourselves and our employees because "eventually things will slow down." However, eventually never comes. In the meantime, our families grow up without us. The message "Work now, family later" is a big swing and a miss. Our message should be "Spend time with family now, and spend time with family later."

The day will never come when various demands stop begging you to take time away from focusing on what's most important. You must choose what to prioritize.

Could prioritizing family mean you might have to give up some entrepreneurial dream? It might. The question is, What do you want in the end?

Too High a Cost

I know too many CEOs who have built "successful" careers at the cost of their families and even their lives.

In just the past few years, we've seen the marriages and families of several business titans go up in smoke. Bill Gates, founder of Microsoft, finalized his divorce in May 2021. Jeff Bezos, founder of Amazon, finalized his divorce in July 2019. Sergey Brin, founder of Twitter, finalized his divorce in 2013. I don't know what happened in these men's lives that led to their divorces, but to me, no amount of work success is worth destroying my family. Is the destruction of your family worth $117 billion? $135 billion? $193 billion? I don't think so.

I came to this conviction more than five decades ago when I worked for another company. A former boss told me, "The most important thing is your job, because your family's going to leave you one day." Yes, he really said that. I will *never* tell someone that the most important thing in their life is their job at Hobby Lobby. Not only is it a false and even wicked statement but also anyone who believes it and follows it stands a very good chance of destroying themselves and their family. God didn't make human beings only for work. What I believed then, I still say today: *Spend time with family now, and spend time with family later, no matter what it might cost your career.*

Spouse before Career

A news article from a few years ago told of a pastor who had given up his faith. "My faith didn't work, God never answered my prayers, and my marriage was a farce," the pastor basically told the reporter.

I don't know the man, and I have no idea what hardships he suffered, but I do know that God may delay answering our prayers for many reasons. I recall a humorous but wise statement once made by Ruth Bell Graham, the wife of the late evangelist Billy Graham: "If God had answered every prayer of mine, I would have married the wrong man seven times." She meant that though God had chosen Billy as her spouse, before she met him she had prayed seven times that the Lord would let her marry someone else—"the wrong man."

I wonder, though, if that pastor had a different problem. His statement, "my marriage was a farce," made me wonder if his prayers went unanswered *because* of his marriage.

"You husbands must give honor to your wives," writes the apostle Peter. "Treat your wife with understanding as you live together. She may be weaker than you are, but she is your equal partner in God's gift of new life. Treat her as you should *so your prayers will not be hindered*" (1 Pet. 3:7 NLT).

How you treat your spouse plays an important role in how God answers (or doesn't answer) your prayers. Christian husbands who fail to honor their wives should *expect* their prayers to go unanswered. That's the Bible's viewpoint, not mine.

Most of us naturally tend to separate our lives by category: work, home, school, church, spirituality. But God recognizes no such artificial separations. He is present in all of life, at all times and in all places.

Early on, Barbara and I set out to have not just a good marriage but a beautiful one. We wanted it to truly glorify God. While both of us have made our share of mistakes, we did one thing right at the very beginning: we intentionally worked for a God-honoring marriage. And by God's grace, that's what we have today.

All married couples face challenges, of course. Only liars claim to have a problem-free marriage! But when problems and challenges arise in marriage, God expects us to keep working at it. If a problem came up at work, you would keep working on it until you solved it, wouldn't you? The same is true in marriage.

If Barbara and I see something going offtrack, we focus on the issue until we learn where we went wrong. We discuss it and ask each other, "What's not working here?" We don't give up until we get the issue straightened out.

I also spend time personally reflecting, again just like at work. When I become aware of some conflict with Barbara, I go to the Scriptures and ask God, "Where am I out of line? Where am I too prideful? Where am I refusing to honor her?" Almost every conflict in marriage boils down to the failure to obey two commands:

- Love one another. (John 13:34)
- Submit to one another. (Eph. 5:21)

When I get offtrack, whether in marriage or in business, the only solution is to get back on track. That's the only way to make good progress in my relationship with Barbara or at work.

Barbara and I also spend lots of time together. My favorite part of each day is having breakfast with her and reading a daily devotional together. The breakfast is nothing fancy, just toast and coffee. She jokes that she makes me bread and water and then sends me out the door, but that's not true. I usually make the coffee.

I try to be home by 5:30 p.m. every day. We take Sunday off to attend church together and spend the afternoon at home. Now that our kids have grown, once a month we go somewhere nearby for a weekend getaway, just to relax, read, and unwind.

Early in our relationship, we both agreed that marriage is for life. We remind ourselves of what Jesus said: "What God has joined together, let no one separate" (Matt. 19:6). Because we take His words and His command seriously, we strive to have a good marriage, one that lasts a lifetime.

If you're married, God wants your marriage to last for life. When you view marriage from this perspective, you look at your problems differently. When you run into hardships or troubles—and all of us do—you don't immediately think, *It looks like our marriage is over.* Rather, because you know that God intends for marriages to last, His goal becomes your goal.

Just as important, you purposefully remember that "with God all things are possible" (Matt. 19:26). No matter how hopeless a situation looks, God can always do the impossible! He specializes in it, in fact. He even asks us, "Is anything too hard for the LORD?" (Gen. 18:14). God first asked that question of Abraham, who had a hard time believing that he and his elderly wife, Sarah, could ever have a son. But because God had promised them a son, God would give them that son—when Abraham was one hundred years old and Sarah ninety.

Is *anything* too hard for the Lord? What about in my marriage? Or in yours? The answer is no.

The twin facts that God wants marriages to last and that nothing is too hard for Him have given Barbara and me great hope. When things get tough, we remember that we have a God who does miracles—and *every* marriage needs a miracle at some point.

Whatever you see as impossible, God sees as an opportunity to show you His power. Why not invite Him into whatever difficulty you face?

Give Up Career for Family?

Some leaders get so focused on the success of their organizations that they neglect the success of their families. Too often, family comes in a distant second. But where does a leader's influence matter the most? At home.

If you have children, do you see them as God does? The Lord has some strong words to say about our kids:

Behold, children are a heritage from the LORD, the fruit of the womb a reward. (Ps. 127:3 ESV)

> The father of a righteous child has great joy;
> a man who fathers a wise son rejoices in him.
> May your father and mother rejoice;
> may she who gave you birth be joyful! (Prov. 23:24–25)

Has not the one God made you? You belong to him in body and spirit. And what does the one God seek? Godly offspring. So be on your guard, and do not be unfaithful to the wife of your youth. (Mal. 2:15)

If you consider yourself a leader but know that one or more of your children have no interest in serving the Lord, you might consider taking a step back from your leadership duties. Give yourself more time to focus on what's happening at home.

Dr. Jim Dobson, founder of Focus on the Family, watched his father do just that. When Jim was six years old, his father felt called to travel the United States as an evangelist. He asked his wife to accompany him while their son stayed home in school. They made the heart-wrenching decision to leave Jim with his aunt—an agonizing separation for the parents and even more so for the little boy.

Jim soon started acting out, causing trouble at school and in the neighborhood. One year later, his parents returned and realized how their decision had devastated their son. Jim's father decided to travel alone and bought a house in Bethany, Oklahoma, so his wife could stay home and raise their son. Between frequent speaking engagements, Jim's dad returned to their home in Bethany.

At age sixteen, Jim started talking back to his mother and ignoring her rules. Late one night after he came home from a party, she called his father, saying only three words: "I need you." Although he was scheduled four years out, he boarded a train, came home, and canceled his entire slate. He found a pastoral position at a church in Texas and moved the family there, all so he could be present for his son's last two years at home.[2]

Decades later, Jim founded Focus on the Family, a worldwide ministry that has impacted millions. He will tell you that it never would have happened if not for his father's sacrificial example of choosing family over career.

No career is more important than your children knowing and serving God. The worst thing you can do is achieve success but lose your family. I see far too many leaders emphasizing business first at the cost of their families, only to end their lives with great net worth but little net worth in regard to their family. Frankly, I would rather Hobby Lobby not exist than for one of my children to fall away from God. No amount of money is worth losing a child's soul. To see my kids serving the Lord is more important to me than all the money, fame, or success in the world.

I've lived eighty years and have met billionaires, presidents, celebrities, and the heads of huge corporations. I can tell you that not one of them is more joyful than the individual who serves the Lord with all their heart. How could I want anything less for our children?

And how, then, could I want anything less for the children of the men and women who work with me at Hobby Lobby?

My parents both lived to see each of their children serving the Lord. On their deathbeds, they both knew the amazing legacy they were leaving behind.

Think ahead to that day when the time comes for you to leave this planet. What thought will grip your mind?

Will it be, How could I have become a billionaire? or rather, How it thrills me to see all my kids walking with God?

What about Employees and Their Families?

God has a definite purpose for sending our way the individuals He has placed in our charge, and it's not simply to help us make a profit. He tells us to be "just and fair" to our workers. He instructs us to remember that we "also have a Master—in heaven" (Col. 4:1 NLT). He commands us to treat our employees right, and He insists that He "has no favorites" (Eph. 6:9 NLT). We have great power as leaders, and great responsibility comes with that power. We can use our authority either to take from our people or to give back to them.

I often say that my marriage and children are more important than my career. If that's true, then the marriages and children of Hobby Lobby's fifty thousand employees must also be more important than their careers. And if *that's* true, then don't I, as the leader, have to do whatever I can to help my colleagues, associates, and employees thrive in their marriages and families?

We build approximately fifty Hobby Lobby stores per year, which means about three hundred new hires come to our headquarters each year for training. I speak at these meetings for about fifteen minutes but not about how to succeed in business. I tell them, "What I've learned over the years is that the easiest thing to do is to be successful in business. For most of us, that's the easy thing. But it's the least important thing."

I then speak of the importance of having a strong marriage and raising children who serve God. *That's* the hard but most critical part. The Bible has much more to say about succeeding with family than succeeding in business. Therefore, more important than our employees' work for Hobby Lobby is their relationships with their family.

We try hard to help our employees succeed in this area. At our corporate headquarters we have a small staff of chaplains whom employees can visit while on the clock. We regularly offer marriage and family classes. We also encourage management staff to take advantage of all-expenses-paid weekend marriage conferences (see chapter 7).

If Hobby Lobby existed only to sell arts and crafts, we would miss out on the far greater work God has for us. We intend to serve and encourage our employees and their families however we can manage it, as together we strive to create a thriving business.

Debbie Kinsey, head of management ministries, illustrates our desire to care for the families of our employees. About eight years ago, her husband passed away from cancer. He and I had become good friends when he was pastoral staff at the church that Barbara and I attended. Four years after his death, Debbie asked her supervisor if she could move out of Oklahoma to be closer to her daughter. The supervisor then mentioned her request to me.

We typically require department heads to work out of our corporate headquarters in Oklahoma City, but I knew

Debbie could benefit from the move. I picked up the phone and called her.

"So, you want to leave me?" I asked her.

"Well, not leave you like *that*," she said. "I just want to be near my daughter."

"Go with my blessing," I told her. "I wouldn't do this for just anybody, but go and live closer to her."

If we don't do whatever we can to equip our people to improve their home lives, then what kind of leaders are we? Can we say we truly serve God if what our employees are doing for us too often takes them away from their families? Perhaps the time has come for us to rethink how their employment with us intersects with their home lives.

Times Have Changed

In one sense, we don't have much choice. Times have changed. The pandemic has altered how people look at their jobs. An article published near the end of 2021 (revealingly titled, "Why Family Friendly Workplaces Are the Answer to the 'Great Resignation'!") quotes research that indicates more than nineteen million workers and counting have quit their jobs since April 2021. Employee attrition is not easing, the article states, but rather, "the impact Covid has had on working families, along with Generation X entering the workplace with a call for greater family friendly related entitlements shows the opposite. . . . The fact is, employees everywhere are re-evaluating their work and care needs and looking to reduce their work life conflict. If employers do not respond, it may mean it is not easy to replace lost talent."[3]

The article also quotes vital research from McKinsey & Co.:

> If the past 18 months have taught us anything, it's that employees crave investment in the human aspects of work. Employees are tired, and many are grieving. They want a renewed and revised sense of purpose in their work. They want social and interpersonal connections with their colleagues and managers. They want to feel a sense of shared identity. Yes, they want pay, benefits, and perks, but more than that they want to feel valued by their organizations and managers. They want meaningful—though not necessarily in-person—interactions, not just transactions.[4]

We at Hobby Lobby are trying to navigate these choppy waters right along with the rest of the country. We certainly don't have all the answers. Those who do our warehouse hiring, for example, tell me that many of our new hires don't stick around for longer than a few weeks or months. Why not? They don't crave higher pay so much as they want frequent time off and more flexible schedules, which is hard to accommodate in a warehouse. We'll figure it out, but it will take time.

I say this because I don't want anyone to think I'm trying to set hard and fast rules for equipping employees to gain a better work/life balance. Nor do I want leaders to feel guilty for situations they can't avoid. But I do want to emphasize the overarching principle: *God wants you to succeed at home first, and He wants the same for those in your charge.*

If we *say* "family first," let's make sure we *act* on it. Let's be sure that it gets folded into the secret sauce. It's one of the sweeter ingredients and one of the most satisfying. It's worth both savoring and celebrating!

Seven

PUT EMPLOYEES FIRST, NOT MONEY

A man at church asked me one Sunday how we could afford to pay our employees seventeen dollars an hour.

"We're fixin' to go to eighteen-fifty," I answered.

His mouth flew open and he exclaimed, "I'd be out of business if I did that!"

The fact is, not too many years ago I would have echoed his words. Today I often say, "Back in the day, I couldn't do what we do today. I couldn't give even fifty dollars back at the beginning. I was in debt, trying to pay the bank and just trying to survive. We're all where we are. But we need to move from where we are to someplace better."

I'm happy to report that my "fixin' to go to eighteen-fifty" statement turned into reality in late December 2021 when our board approved the proposed pay hike. We won't go out of business because of it, but we didn't approve such a big change lightly either. We know the cost; it's not cheap. We crunched the numbers, and the pay hike comes to $70 million, not counting employees who already make eighteen dollars an hour. We need to bump up their wages too because they've been with us for two years. We figure the total cost for this wage increase will land somewhere in the neighborhood of $100 million.

"That's a lot of money!" someone says, and it is. But I believe it's the right thing to do. I also believe God will bless us afterward, but not *because* we increased our employees' minimum wage—as if we could *earn* His blessing through our efforts. God doesn't work like that. He never says, "I tell you what. You give one dollar, and I'll give you ten in return. Deal?" Nobody can earn, buy, steal, or force God's blessings. He gives them to us out of pure grace.

Still, I think our employees will appreciate the pay hike. I also hope they will reflect their appreciation in good work habits. Most of our people, I believe, try to do the very best they can because they know we want to do our very best for them.

As I said, however, our care hasn't always been this abundant. And I see two main reasons that help to explain why not.

Reason One: We Lacked the Ability

Where we are today is *not* where we started. We haven't always been able to pay our employees as well as we do now. Our ability to raise wages and provide other benefits has been evolving and growing over many years.

For most of Hobby Lobby's history, I paid only what I could afford (and then, often just barely). Back then, I was just trying to make payroll. That was my entire focus.

I've already described how, in the early days, I ran Hobby Lobby like other businesses—embracing debt, betting next year's payments on last year's sales. Even after we had a dozen stores, we continued taking out loans. We purchased each year's inventory on loan, assuming that our profit from the year before predicted what we could afford the following year.

We nearly went under from taking out loans we couldn't afford. God eventually brought us out of the darkness and allowed the company to survive, but it was touch and go for many months.

Not until the last decade or so has Hobby Lobby reached the place where it could even consider the kinds of company benefits that we offer today. So if you can't yet afford to pay your full-time workers a minimum wage of $18.50 an hour, don't feel either bad or guilty. We didn't get there until recently.

At the same time, as you read this chapter, I encourage you to imagine a very different scenario that could exist for you in the not-too-distant future. Picture a time when you can begin figuring out how to creatively bless your employees in ways that not only make sense for your business or organization but also let your people know "This place really cares for me!"

Reason Two: I Lacked the Heart

One day, after we had started sending large monetary gifts to world evangelism projects, I had yet another divine episode. I'll never forget what I heard God say: *I've put these employees in your charge.*

It hit me with sledgehammer force that if I intended to send resources abroad to minister to families around the globe, I also had to do everything in my power to care for our employees. God had brought each one of them to Hobby Lobby. How could I do less for them than I wanted to do for people on the other side of the world whom I would never even meet? This was another pivotal moment for Hobby Lobby.

I used to struggle with how to carve up the financial pie: Give it to missions and help people prepare for eternity, or use it to improve the lives of those who work for Hobby Lobby? Before the Lord spoke to my heart about our employees, I clearly valued giving to missions ahead of caring for our people. I'm glad to say I no longer struggle with this issue.

The Bible says, "Do not withhold good from those to whom it is due, when it is in your power to act" (Prov. 3:27). It hasn't always been in my power to help our employees as I can now, but I strongly sense God has continued to say to me, *You take care of your people first. I'm not asking you to do missions work at their expense. You take good care of your people.*

When I do that, I believe we'll end up with more, not

less, to give so that we can give even more to our people. Some of our giving may not make financial sense at the time, but we've seen God bless such giving time and again. I believe with all my heart that if I give our people more and if I'll take good care of them, God will take care of the other part.

I think I have good reason for that belief. While it took us fifty years to be able to give X amount, we went from X to 2X in two years. It's a total God thing. I believe this ability to give generously developed over time, in a gradual, evolutionary way. While I have a general sense of how it came about, I can't completely explain it. But however it happened, I'm glad it did.

Today, I'm not afraid to say, "If I have only a dollar, I'm going to give it to our people and not to missions." I wouldn't have said that years ago. Over time, my desire to take care of *our* people first grew stronger and stronger. I owe it to them to pay them well to the best of my ability. Again, I hear Scripture ringing in my ears: "'Do not muzzle an ox while it is treading out the grain,' and 'The worker deserves his wages'" (1 Tim. 5:18).

As God continues to bless us, He seems to increasingly put into our spirits a strong desire to take care of our people. I want our employees to know how we feel about them. I want them to see that we care about them. And I don't want them killing themselves for the sake of a job.

Even so, just as we owe our people a fair wage, so they owe us a fair day's work. We have a duty to pay them well, and they have a duty to give Hobby Lobby their best effort and labor. It goes both ways. We both have a responsibility to one another.

I can't *make* anyone work hard, of course, and I reject the idea of threatening, berating, shaming, manipulating, or pressuring employees to work harder. If worse comes to worse, as a last resort I certainly *will* fire someone. But before then, we try to work with underperforming employees to find out why they're struggling and to see how we might be able to help them. We want all our people to succeed, to win, to thrive.

To that end, we have several resources designed to give employees the assistance they may need. I'd like to describe a few of them to you, not to brag about Hobby Lobby but to give you a few ideas of what might work for you and your own associates and employees. I would love to hear if any of the following brief descriptions spark some creative ideas of your own that we could use at Hobby Lobby. If so, please let me know!

What Shows Genuine Concern?

Today, more than ever, I want to do everything I can to help our employees.

That's why our stores close at 8:00 p.m. None of our competitors do that.

That's why we're closed on Sunday. None of our competitors do that.

That's why our stores are open for just sixty-six hours each week. None of our competitors do that.

That's why our minimum wage for full-time workers, as of January 1, 2022, is $18.50 an hour. Who else does that?

We also try to help our employees thrive in several other ongoing ways. I won't present an exhaustive list, but allow me to highlight a few initiatives that have worked very well for us.

Once a month on our Oklahoma City campus, any employee who lives in the area, along with their spouse, can come for a free all-day life enrichment workshop. One month the workshop focuses on marriage, the next month it offers help and guidance on raising children. These seminars might be taught by one of our own chaplains, or we might bring in outside experts to give us their best insights. The room normally used for these sessions has a capacity of approximately two hundred persons, and I'm told it typically gets pretty full.

We have a special perk for all our salaried managerial employees working in stores across the country. They have an opportunity to attend a first-class weekend retreat on marriage enrichment, most often a "Weekend to Remember" event hosted by FamilyLife. We pay all employee expenses, from the flight to the hotel room to meals to the conference fee to incidentals. We pay for the entire weekend. We see it as a great investment.

A staff of full-time chaplains (currently five) works out of our headquarters. Any employee with a nonwork-related problem can visit a chaplain at any time, on the clock, to get counsel and help. Employees can't bring up conflicts with supervisors or disputes with coworkers or discuss job complaints, but just about anything else is fair game. Many of our people ask for a chaplain's help with problems they're having at home. Probably the biggest troubles, our chaplains tell me, involve children or anger management. Sometimes we may send hurting individuals to other ministries in town that might be better equipped to provide longer term solutions to serious problems, such as alcohol or drugs.

Through the chaplain's office we also run a program called Shared Harvest, a monthly frozen food distribution program available to all employees working at our main campus.

While I've never told anyone to bring their problems to work, I want them to see an attitude in us that communicates, "What can we do to help you? Is there something we can do?" We *don't* want them hearing us say, "Hey, get busy! We need you to make us more money."

Also at our headquarters we operate a medical clinic, fully staffed with medical professionals, including nurses and physicians. The clinic even has an MRI machine, which already has caught some serious physical conditions among our employees that otherwise might have gone undetected. The clinic is part of the health insurance program we make available to employees.

We do things like these because we care about our people. We also want them to know that God cares for them far more than we do. Since most of our employees have heard me say that God owns our business (see chapter 1), I try to follow His example as much as I can. Because

God takes care of us, in a far lesser sense I try to take care of our people. I tell my leaders the same thing: "Take care of your people. Understand where they are, and try to do whatever you can for them."

I encourage you to do the same. Ask God to give you a heart for your people. Think creatively how you can serve and care for them. It's another critical ingredient in the secret sauce.

A Growing Circle

As God continues to bless us, we also want to bless a growing circle of men and women from outside of Hobby Lobby. About seven or eight times a year, we hold a two-day seminar for business leaders and CEOs. During these meetings, we focus not only on good business practices but also on generosity and creating a legacy that lives on for decades and generations.

My coauthor and friend, Bill High, usually emcees these meetings. He typically interviews me about Hobby Lobby's history and the key lessons I've learned along the way (although I admit that I often don't make his job easy). When I wander off the beaten path, which happens not infrequently, Bill patiently and expertly brings me back to the question. We also open our sessions to questions from participants, giving them an opportunity to dig further into the weeds of whatever topic we're discussing.

Bill and I first started holding these workshops about a decade ago, about ten years after we got acquainted through his work in generosity and donor-advised funds. Bill is a former lawyer who now spends most of his time working with and consulting with families to help them create thriving family legacies and to see lives changed by Jesus. "What would happen," Bill asks, "if generosity became less about transactions and more about transformation? What if generosity became less about dollar amounts and more about a way to pass on families' values and stories?" Our two-day event powerfully impacts many participants, often making a big difference in their lives and in their work.

I recently received a note from a CEO who attended one of our events. "Here are a few of the things that I took away," he wrote, listing several examples. He then declared, "We're going to do these better."

In one way, his note summarizes not only what we try to do in these workshops but also what we try to do for our Hobby Lobby employees. As much as possible, I want to help them "do things better" so that they can build better lives, experience more joy, and find their core purpose. Hobby Lobby isn't just about arts and crafts; it's about improving human lives on multiple levels.

Never Lose Good People

I'm sure no employer wants to lose good workers, but we've adopted that desire as an official attitude: "Never lose good people." We never *ever* want to lose good people. Sometimes, of course, we can't help it.

A man who did a great job for us once told me he was leaving Hobby Lobby after another company promised to double his salary. He returned to us after two weeks. He came back, he explained, because people at the new workplace habitually cursed him out. He missed the more positive environment we've tried hard to create, and we felt glad to have him back. While things don't always play out like this, neither is his situation particularly unusual.

Good people who express their intention to go elsewhere are worth trying to keep around. I sometimes say to them, "You tell me you're going to company X. Do you know where you're going? Have you seen their P&L?"

"No, I didn't see their P&L."

"Well, they lost two million last year. You're about to put your family's life in that company. There are other companies out there as good or better than Hobby Lobby, but at least know where you're going if you want to leave here." I honestly hate losing good people.

A man who worked for a huge company once serviced one of our stores. "I can't believe this," he told me. "These people have been here five, eight, ten, fifteen years. We *never* keep ours longer than a few months. How do you do it? At our place, six months is about it."

I'd want to ask that man how his company treats its people. I'm guessing the answer to that question probably has something to do with its ability to retain quality employees. When you include this ingredient in your own secret sauce, your employees can easily taste the difference.

Care Like He Does

While we never push our Christian faith on anyone, our people know that our care for them comes out of our love for God and that our love for God comes out of His love for us. Scripture says, "We love because he [God] first loved us" (1 John 4:19). This is our life.

It's hard for me to see how anyone could be a part of this company and *not* know that we care about them. We care about their salary. We care about their hours. We care about *them*.

At certain times we step out in front of an audience and talk explicitly about Christ. We let audience members know that we love Jesus and that our love for Him generates our love for them. We often miss the target, but at least everyone knows what we strive to do.

We started bringing comanagers to our corporate headquarters in 2009 as part of their orientation and training. We want them to know this company and our culture. I've already mentioned that at these meetings I encourage our newest comanagers to serve their employees and to prioritize their families above their work. Immediately afterward, our vice president, Ken Haywood, and our warehouse manager, Bill Woody, speak about who we are and what we value.

The main thing I want our new hires to catch is a desire to take care of the people in their stores. I want our supervisors and store managers to know that we care about them, and then I want them to come together to do something for their employees that says, "We care about you." That's the primary lesson I want them to absorb in their short time at headquarters. At the very top of our list is putting people first. Our men and women are far more important than this business.

What It's All About

I recently turned eighty years old. Several hundred employees sent me birthday cards. (I'm pretty sure my staff put them up to it.) I brought a bunch of those cards home.

It means a lot to me that employees say, "I'm a different person today because I watched you serve the Lord." I'll keep those cards around for a long time and reread them periodically to remind me of what Hobby Lobby is all about.

Even when it's not my birthday, I occasionally get letters and notes from employees around the country, thanking us for this benefit or that event. I received a letter not long ago that said, "I'm at Hobby Lobby because of what I've seen around here." That means a great deal to me. Notes and letters like this let me know that we're doing at least a few things right. They help me see that our people really do know that we care for them.

In the end, it's all about helping and encouraging others. It's about following Scripture and trying to obey what the Lord says. We want God's Word to direct our lives, our business, and our families. And we want our people to know that God's love lies at the center of everything we're trying to accomplish. We've seen some great things happen over the years through various departments and ministries at Hobby Lobby!

And so I wonder, *What could God do through* your *leadership at* your *organization?* Regardless of your business or industry, remember that the people on your team have souls. Each one of them needs you to care for them.

Personal Care over Official Titles

Our leaders at Hobby Lobby work hard to make their people feel appreciated, cared for, and valued. At meetings involving many levels of employees, for example, you'll see heads of departments, VPs, frontline employees, the CFO, and others all sitting arm to arm, working together without much concern for rank. Our executives have job titles, but they don't flaunt them.

We work hard to respect our people and give them the authority to run within their designated areas of authority. They tell us this means a lot to them and makes them feel empowered and valued. They don't want high fives but rather to be respected for what they bring to the table. It's an important way for us to show our genuine care for them.

Not long ago we hired a hard-core security professional who for seventeen years had worked for a public company. The company was very title driven, and it bothered him that he had no big title. "If you can get your head past that," his boss, Jeanne, told him, "after you've been here about three months, you'll realize it doesn't matter. You're not going to be respected because of your title. You're going to be respected for what you're bringing to the table—and you're bringing a ton to the table."

About six weeks into his employment, he told Jeanne about a meeting he'd attended. It surprised him that none of those present announced their titles. One said, "I'm from distribution," another said, "I'm from technology," and so on. One outside vendor in the room couldn't even tell who outranked who.

"That never would have happened at my old company," our startled new employee said. "We would've spent fifteen minutes on people announcing their pedigrees." That day, it suddenly clicked for him that our people wanted to hear from *him*. They cared for *him*. They wanted *him* to feel valued because they did highly value him.

Caring for your people is an integral part of the secret sauce that sets up your organization for success. When you bless others by genuinely caring for them, you invite God to do something extraordinary in the world through your work.

eiGHT

DEFER TO YOUR PEOPLE, DON'T JUST LISTEN TO THEM

Do you come from a work culture in which "what the boss says, goes"? I know I did. I grew up in the South in the 1940s where "Yes, sir," and "Yes, ma'am" were the only appropriate responses to elders. As a worker, I learned to keep quiet and do what I was told. Some of my bosses were dictators. While they taught me to honor authority, they didn't help me prepare to be a leader.

When I became a leader myself, I adopted their dictatorial style. Common business practice at the time was "he's the boss; do what he says," and I accepted that attitude without question. I often took the approach, "Now that I'm the boss, you need to do what I say." At times I didn't care whether my employees knew where I intended to take them or whether they were on board with me. But I soon realized if my employees adopted such an attitude, it would kill my business.

Today we hear all the time, "Hire people smarter than you," which I consider excellent advice. But when I see how some of us lead, I want to ask, "If the people you hire are smarter than you, then why don't you listen to them? If they're so great, then shouldn't you want to hear what they have to say?"

It goes beyond listening, of course. All successful leaders need to develop the leadership skills of those on their team, and one of the best ways to do that is to ask for their good ideas, to really listen to those ideas, and to defer to their judgment wherever appropriate. It means a great deal to young leaders to hear the boss say, "That's a great idea! Let's do that. It's much better than what I had in mind." When you yield to a great approach suggested by subordinates, you build their confidence and create strong leadership for the future.

Encourage Them to Challenge You

One of our employees came to us from a dying company. She worked for a grocery store chain, family-owned for seventy-five years. It had a long legacy of good leadership. When the owners got ready to retire, they decided to transition the company from private to public ownership.

They brought in new executives from the outside to make the transition. The new executives told the staff, in essence, "If you've been here longer than five years, you have nothing new to bring to the table. Your ideas are obsolete." They listened to none of the long-term employees.

The company quickly started to decline. The board brought in consulting firms to try to save the business, but the advice they got simply drove the company further into the red. Finally, the company declared bankruptcy.

The firm overseeing the corporate dissolution sent in a chief restructuring officer to oversee the bankruptcy. That officer immediately saw the problem. He told my employee, "This is the first time I've seen an organization in which the employees of lower rank understood the business better than those above them. They could have rescued the company if only the leaders had listened to them."

If you want to lead well, you must listen to your people and give them the freedom to challenge you. The scariest words an employee can say to me are "Okay, if that's what you want." These words indicate my colleague knows I'm about to go down a dangerous path, but they don't dare to try stopping me. If an employee ever speaks those words to me, I'll immediately reply, "No, no, no—tell me what you think." I know they'll have a few points I haven't considered. After hearing them out, sometimes I'll counter by noting something they haven't considered. But at times they'll alter my position by bringing up a crucial factor that had never even occurred to me.

I need every leader at Hobby Lobby to be frank with me. I don't always see what they see, and for that reason I don't always know what's best. I must hear from others, especially when their views differ from my own. The CEO can (and does) make mistakes as easily as anyone else.

This ingredient in the secret sauce can taste a little sour or even bitter to some leaders, but when it gets mixed in with all the other components, the result is nothing less than amazing. Once you've tasted the end product, you'll never go back to anything else.

The Elephant in the Room

Have you ever been the elephant in the room? You know, where you're so big and important that your opinion holds sway above everyone else's? When an elephant leaves a room, everyone knows it. I don't want to be the elephant. When I leave the room, I don't want anyone to know it, to the best of my ability.

That said, if something should go catastrophically wrong tomorrow at Hobby Lobby because I'm not here, I *am* the elephant. Since I don't want to be the elephant, I'm trying to make sure I don't have to be here for the company to continue running smoothly.

That's why I have my grandson-in-law Joe Fallon at my side for much of each day. For the last five years, I've been teaching him everything I know about merchandising. When I leave, he'll take over my merchandising role and nothing will change at Hobby Lobby in that key aspect of the company. Nothing will fall apart.

I recognize that I'm not smart enough to call all the shots. You're not that smart either. No one is. Every decision requires two-way dialogue. I encourage my employees to challenge me, and I change direction at times because of their counsel. When appropriate, I defer to their judgment or opinion.

Randy Betts, our senior vice president of store operations, once suggested that we send out seasonal items to each store based on how much they sold for that season during the previous year. He pointed out that different regions have differing seasonal needs. Chicago, for example, sells the most St. Patrick's Day merchandise of any area in the United States. Customers in the north start purchasing spring items much later than those in the south because for them, spring arrives later. He encouraged me to start a new zoning system for our stores.

I didn't buy the idea at first, but Randy kept bringing it up. Once we tried it, it saved us millions of dollars. It also allowed stores to focus on their bestselling seasonal products (and it doesn't disrupt our ratio-to-sales system).

About fifteen years ago, Ken Haywood challenged me to consider creating a layout room at our headquarters to use as a model for all our stores. At the time, we let store managers decide for themselves how to display merchandise. Ken thought corporate should make all layout decisions and send stores those instructions. As a former store manager, I had loved the freedom to figure out on my own how to display merchandise. I wanted our managers to have the same freedom. It took five years of Ken suggesting the idea before we decided to try it. We took it slow and first tested it with a few stores. It worked so well and brought us so many more sales that the layout room is now standard procedure.

People who work for you have good ideas. No leader has to implement every new idea suggested, but we must create a culture that welcomes new ideas and gives them a fair hearing. If nobody on your team feels free to challenge you, then you have a huge problem—and that problem is you. You're the elephant in the room.

Listening matters. Hire smart, honest people, and then listen to them. When their ideas make good sense, implement them, give them the credit, and celebrate the resulting success. If you want your organization to thrive and reach new heights, it's the only option.

Courageous Conversations

The idea of one person challenging the ideas of another assumes some type of conflict. While many leaders see absence of conflict as a good thing, it can in fact signal real danger.

In *The Five Dysfunctions of a Team*, Patrick Lencioni lists "fear of conflict" as one of the five key dysfunctions.[1] Conflict allows us to honestly discuss differences of opinion, regardless of who's the boss.

The authors of another book, *Great by Choice*, describe Intel's recipe for success. The firm began in 1969 by identifying several of its key ingredients, one of which was "practice constructive confrontation." Leaders encouraged employees to "argue and debate regardless of rank, and then commit once a decision is made—disagree and commit."[2]

Intel discontinued its core business of producing memory chips in 1985 and switched to microprocessors, a decision that made Intel a household name. But long before the change, the firm's leaders put communication processes in place that allowed it to smoothly make such a drastic change. The leadership welcomed open debate in which employees could identify company weaknesses and suggest new solutions.

What would need to change at your organization for your employees to think of you as their Chief Encouragement Officer? Can you say, kindly, what needs to be said without shying away from difficult conversations? Do you have a greater interest in producing a positive outcome than avoiding discomfort? What would need to change for your leaders to feel more comfortable engaging you in open debate?

Lencioni observes that conflict often comes from a healthy trust in and passion for an organization's mission. He also points out the difference between constructive and destructive conflict. Destructive conflict attacks a person while constructive conflict critiques ideas. "Ideological conflict is limited to concepts and ideas and avoids personality-focused, mean-spirited attacks," Lencioni writes. Teams that take part in constructive conflict "discuss and resolve issues more quickly and completely than others, and they emerge from heated debates with no residual feelings or collateral damage, but with an eagerness and readiness to take on the next important issue."[3]

Courageous conversations never attack individuals but rather debate the strength of their ideas. Do your people feel comfortable having such courageous conversations with you?

The 51:49 Principle

How I make decisions at Hobby Lobby is no secret. I sit down with others, and we talk through the pros and cons of each proposal.

And that's it. It really is that simple.

We think through what will happen, both benefits and costs, if we pull the trigger on some idea. Then we ask the opposite. If we don't make this change, what are our possible benefits and costs? I talk the matter through with whoever is responsible for the change and most affected by it. We weigh our options together and choose whatever appears to offer the greatest benefit. Sometimes my opinion prevails; sometimes I defer to others. The key thing is not who had the idea but which option makes the most sense.

Most of our decisions are not 100 percent for one side but more like 60:40. We have found it a tremendous help to decide ahead of time that we will always choose the greatest benefit, even if the decision is split 51:49. We always choose the greatest potential gain, even if it offers just a bit more.

We do this, for example, when deciding whether to adopt some new software program. Our IT department has an entire team of developers who continually research and test new software. If they find something that seems to work better for our store registers, we evaluate it. It may be better, but by how much? Is it worth the time and cost of training twenty thousand cashiers on how to use the new system? If it is, then we bite the bullet and make the change because we estimate it will save us ten clicks on every checkout, which will save us thirty seconds, which will get customers through the lines faster. If it is not worth it, we discard the idea as 49:51—a good idea but not good enough to implement.

At times we have made what we thought was a 60:40 decision, but as we continued to discuss it, we realized we had it backward. And so we backpedaled. We reversed course and decided not to do something that earlier we had chosen to do. As a leader, I try to avoid reversing decisions, but sometimes you can't escape it. In those situations, you swallow your pride, admit your miscalculation, and change course. You trust both the process and your colleagues.

Create Ownership

If you want your potential leaders to become excellent leaders, never undermine whatever authority you give them. Otherwise, the employees who report to them will start to wonder who's really running the show.

Do your best to develop a culture of deference. At Hobby Lobby, deference means that in a clash of opinions, whoever is in charge stays in charge.

Some years ago, a serious issue arose in a department at our corporate office. The manager asked our general counsel, Peter Dobelbower, for advice, which Peter gave him. When the manager made a different decision, Peter felt concerned. He wrote a letter to the department's senior vice president, saying, "I don't know if you've seen this, but here is the situation." Peter repeated his advice but ended the letter, "As always, I defer to your decision."

As general counsel, Peter could easily give orders. But at Hobby Lobby, we let each leader run their own department. We speak up when we believe we need to speak up, knowing that at the end of the day, each leader makes their own decision.

Peter owns the legal department. He was our original general counsel. We had no job description for him when he arrived. The CFO simply said, "Your office is right down the hall." Peter created the job on his own. In time, he became responsible for human resources and now other departments as well. He owns his department but not any other department. He might see a potential legal issue looming in someone else's department, but he chooses to give advice and let the department leaders make their own decisions.

The same holds true throughout our company. Randy owns store operations, Bill owns warehousing, Jeanne owns IT, and so on. Because I trust the people I have put in charge, I don't micromanage their departments. I stay in the weeds where I am anointed, and I let them handle everything else. I want them to sense ownership of their department—and the only way to create ownership is by giving them full authority to fulfill their responsibilities. I don't want to get in the way of their leadership.

Giving senior leaders this kind of ownership comes with a cost. We all make mistakes; nobody does their job perfectly. At times I have thought, *Why did they do that? I wish they had asked me.* Then I remember the other ninety-nine great decisions they made that I didn't have to bother with, thank God, and I see the wisdom of giving them the freedom to make mistakes.

Communication is key in creating ownership. Let your people know ahead of time what kinds of decisions you want to weigh in on. I know almost nothing about IT, so I weigh in on very few decisions there. This is why you need people you can absolutely trust.

Giving leaders ownership of their departments has created an incredible energy around their jobs. They come into work motivated, knowing their decisions carry real weight, and they have power to make a tremendous difference in the company. Creating ownership among leaders also has allowed us to scale Hobby Lobby from one store to nearly a thousand. Any organization that wants to grow must foster ownership among its leadership.

Put trustworthy people in leadership positions, and then give them the authority they need to operate successfully. If you try to micromanage everything, you will fail. And if you keep undermining their authority, they will find it impossible to establish ownership (and the really good ones will leave). Creating ownership never says, "Whatever the boss says, goes." Rather, we listen to one another, recognizing that each leader is in charge of their own area of responsibility. I insist that we have this key ingredient in our sauce.

Leadership Is Like a Train

All leaders need their people to board the train they're driving. You do too. If they don't get on board with you, you'll fail. Deciding to move ahead with some significant course of action that they don't endorse is like stepping off the train and stepping in front of it. You'll get flattened.

Talk to your people before making a big decision, making sure they are on board with you. If you do so, they will give you grace if your choice turns out to be wrong. After all, they made the decision too! But if you strike out on your own and get it wrong, they will see you made a mistake, lose confidence in you, and hesitate to follow your leadership—especially if they've seen you make several lone ranger mistakes.

The train often flattens those who want to be the hero. Maybe a leader sees their idea as the best, and so they run ahead and implement it without discussing it with anyone. I saw this happen recently. One of our leaders spoke with no one before moving ahead on an idea. No one on his team had agreed with the idea or even knew about it, and it was a bad idea. The train ran over him. If he had just spoken with even a few of his team members, none of this would have happened.

Had that would-be hero just spoken with me, I could have killed the idea before it killed anyone else. Usually, the hero doesn't know this, this, or that, while I *do* know this, this, and that. Had the hero spoken with me first, he would've ended up looking much better. Instead, he wound up looking as if he just got squashed by a train. Most heroes, I've discovered, don't generally want to be on a team. That, fortunately, is the total opposite of what we typically have around here. We don't have many lone ranger leaders, and the few would-be heroes tend to change over time or leave. Hobby Lobby highly values a team-based approach, and everyone knows it. It's an integral part of our secret sauce.

Don't get in front of the engine. Make sure your people are on board with your plans before you get the train moving. If you don't, it may run over you (and I'd say you deserve it). If your people don't want to board a train going in your chosen direction, don't say, "We're going there anyway." Have some conversations. Try to persuade rather than coerce them. If it's a good idea, others will see its benefits and eventually hop on board. If it's a bad idea, well, it'll be better for you and your organization if that train never leaves the station.

You've Got This

Let your leaders know you have confidence in them. Frequently tell them, "You've got this." This says to them, "I trust you." Micromanagement of subordinates erodes their confidence.

Suppose Bill from the warehouse comes to me and says, "What can I do for you?"

"Bill," I say, "you're doing it! I can't believe we're doing 20 percent more business and that you managed to get more trucks out here. Nobody can get trucks right now, but you're making it happen."

I trusted Peter Dobelbower, our general counsel, when agitators came from the outside and tried to unionize us. We beat them worse than they'd ever been beaten in their history, and that was before we instituted our higher minimum wage. Only 17 percent of our workers voted to unionize while 83 percent said a loud no! If it happened today, I think we'd get an even larger margin. And so I say to Peter, "You've got this! I trust you. I don't know what you know because you spend countless hours a week thinking about these issues."

When our abortifacient case went to the US Supreme Court in 2014 (see chapter 2), we had to decide who would represent us. Peter said to me, "I think we ought to do such and such."

"You've got this," I told him. And we won our case.

You need people you trust in critical positions. That's the key. Do you consider them trustworthy? They'll make mistakes, of course; we all do. Ask yourself, *Are they mistakes of doing or not doing?* If they're mistakes of not doing, I admit I'm not always very kind.

Never give leaders responsibility without also giving them the authority required to fulfill that responsibility. Responsibility without authority never works. The people you're working with must know that you trust them. They need to hear you say, "You've got this." They need to hear, "I'm the captain of the ship, but this is your deck. It's your decision."

This is the way, I believe, to develop excellent leaders. Listen to them, defer to their judgment whenever possible, and watch the excitement grow.

PART THREE

COMMONSENSE PRACTICES

NINE NINE NINE NINE NINE NINE NINE NINE NINE NINE NINE NINE NINE N

Nine

REMEMBER YOUR ONE THING, NOT THE SHINY THINGS

Many of us feel a great temptation to try to be great at many things. We deceive ourselves into saying, "I can do this too."

How many times have we seen organizations fail because they tried to pursue too many things at once? They moved away from their core, their identity.

God gave me one talent, not five. I buy and sell merchandise; that's my *one thing*. God made me a merchant, and I'm pretty good at that one thing. When you drill down, our profit at Hobby Lobby comes from buying and selling merchandise. Period. Our sole purpose, whether as employees or as a company or as ministry partners, is to make a profit as a great merchant. But in order to do that, we need a great organization.

When I worked at TG&Y, my supervisors would come in and say, "David, do you know the most important aspect of being a leader?"

Every time, their answer stayed the same: "Organization, organization, organization." They drilled this philosophy into me, and rightly so. A leader's most important role is to build a great organization. Even the president of the United States first carefully selects his cabinet. He surrounds himself with great people in order to lead well. Great leaders know to first surround themselves with great people.

As CEO at Hobby Lobby, I have selected senior vice presidents to run key areas of the company—finance, distribution, and so on. These senior VPs have now been with us an average of twenty-seven years. When they first came on board, we had lots of conversations to get on the same page. We talked about treating people well, doing business with integrity, and more until I was certain our leaders shared my values. Today, I have full trust in every senior VP—which makes my job as CEO easy. They require hardly any supervision.

Since they make my job as CEO so easy, I decided to give myself a second job. I also serve as the senior vice president of marketing, which means I spend the majority of my time in merchandising. Because I want to contribute where I bring the greatest value, I work as a merchandiser. If the most important thing for Hobby Lobby is buying and selling merchandise, then I need to spend the bulk of my time on my one thing.

What is your one thing? To succeed as a leader, set up a great organization that allows you to focus on your gifting and not get distracted.

An Early Love

I first realized that I loved merchandising when I started working for TG&Y during my junior and senior years of high school. I simply loved it. I looked forward to going to the store and seeing how I could take an item from a side counter, put it on an end counter, buy twice as much, and earn three times as much. I loved trying to get the right item in the right space.

Being a merchant intrigued me. What could I do with displays? How could I discover what sells and what doesn't? Why does this work but not that? I studied it all. At one time, TG&Y operated nine hundred stores in twenty-nine states. The chain opened in 1935 and closed in 2001. When the company went from dime stores to family centers, it offered me a manager's position at an eighty-thousand-square-foot store. "It's yours," they told me. "You can do whatever you want with it."

That, by the way, is why the company no longer exists. It had no operational rules for managers, no systems in place—nothing was simple. While that approach provided me with a great place to experiment, it eventually killed the company. TG&Y's one thing should have been being a great merchant. But they couldn't be great at merchandising because their lack of organization caused them to lose focus.

I decided to build a pet department and hired thirteen people to run it. As I continued to experiment with a variety of departments, I eventually thought, *No one does arts and crafts right*. The big box stores have a little of everything but specialize in nothing. *Someone needs to be the category killer of crafts*, I thought. I decided, over time, that I wanted to be that person.

At the time, I looked at my store's little craft department and decided to expand it. It was a start, but where I began was *not* what God had for me long-term. It was just a beginning place to get us to where we are now. I didn't start in this business by saying, "I'm going to create Hobby Lobby."

When we finally opened Hobby Lobby, we had only crafts. Bit by bit, we began to add other departments. First, we added art, then frames. Today, we like to say that we have twelve stores under one roof.

Decades ago, the ma-and-pa shops wanted to show customers how to do various crafts. Even back then, I said, "I'm going to be the merchant. If someone wants a class, they can have a class, but I want to be a great merchant." That's my one thing.

The Best at Being Better

Every organization must know its identity. What is your purpose? Where do you fall among competitors? Hobby

Lobby is in the "better" business. I often talk to my buyers about good, better, and best and tell them, "We're in the better business." If "good" is the bottom and "best" is the top, we're in the middle at "better." We offer quality products that aren't terribly expensive or high-end. We don't focus on the best, and we don't want to be just good. We're better—where 80 percent of the sales are.

I tell our buyers that we want to be "the best at being better." And what does it mean to be the best? Best does not always mean having the greatest selection. We have a smaller selection of art supplies than our main competitor, but we buy our art, our paints, and our brushes direct from the factory so we can sell them all at half price every other week. We don't have to offer all the major brands.

Our competitors may have more brands and a larger selection of art items than we do, but I doubt they have more sales than we do. We think our art department is the best at being better, not because we have the largest selection but because of how we operate that department. Customers come to us because of price and quality. This philosophy carries over to all our departments.

Consider our fabric department. One of our competitors has a larger selection of fabric, but we probably have more sales than they do. Why? We don't overstock, so our merchandise constantly turns over. We also have fabric designed by our own art department, unique merchandise that customers can get nowhere else.

We don't think there's a better floral department than ours. You'll see the same thing in our party department.

Granted, competitor party stores carry a bigger selection, but if customers need crafts along with their party supplies, we're a one-stop shop. And at Hobby Lobby they also find better prices. *That's* why we think we can become the very best at being better in almost every department.

We've also found it easier to be the best at better because we have lower employee turnover than our competitors. We don't have to keep training new people. Most of our store employees work in the department that most interests them, so they stick around. Our merchandise managers each have about six others working for them, all of whom must become the best at every subcategory they oversee. That's how we operate. We focus on being the best at better. As a result, we have great sales.

I don't want Hobby Lobby to be just another craft store. To succeed we must have a clear reason for being, and to accomplish that we must remain focused. We continually ask ourselves, How do we stay (or become) the best at being better?

To make our desire a reality, we focus more on what our customers want than on what our competitors do. I want to do what's right for our customers, regardless of what happens in our competitors' stores.

Put the Customer First

Hobby Lobby carries approximately a hundred thousand items, including seasonal merchandise. We have about one hundred buyers. We break down our purchasing to twelve departments, with twelve merchandise managers, each with about a half-dozen buyers on their team. Each buyer makes decisions for subcategories in their department, such as feathers or pom-poms in the craft department. I tell all of our buyers, "If you want to know what to buy, study, study, study. And follow the customers. That will tell you what to do." We have great buyers who do a fantastic job.

If you want to be the best, you listen to your customers. You observe what they buy, see where they're going, attend trade shows. You read everything about your little world. For example, if you're focused on buying party items, then you ought to be pretty good at knowing what to buy. You buy these five colors of cake toppers, in these sizes, at these price points. If you keep your head where it ought to be, you learn an incredible amount. Your customers will tell you what to buy.

We also carefully watch the numbers. We know who runs the very best art department in all our stores. We can't have a thousand stores calling the art department, but I can tell a buyer to call a specific person at store number X because we know that person is sharp and knows what the customer wants. Our buyers learn a lot about our customers through our stores' department heads.

We are not here to create trends. We *never* create a trend. Ever. We observe what customers want, and we give it to them. We do not try to convince them to buy something new that we think is wonderful.

Five years ago at Christmas, nobody sold little trucks with trees in the back. Today, we sell thousands of them a year. But we're not the trendsetter. We could never say, "We're responsible for macramé. We're responsible for scrapbooking." Instead, we're trend *identifiers* who capitalize on those trends.

It all goes back to good, better, best. We're in the better business. We can't be everything to everybody. We make everyone's job a lot harder if we offer more selection than what 80 percent of our customers say they want.

If we left this ingredient out of our secret sauce, we'd end up with a product that costs too much and couldn't be sustained. A laser focus on our one thing is crucial to our success.

The One Thing and Your Anointing

My one thing is the retail strategy of buying and selling—the general work of being a great merchandiser. God gifted me as a merchant. Through retail, I can make a profit, part of which we can give away to impact people's lives for eternity. That's my purpose, my calling.

But I still need an anointing.

We don't often use the word *anointing* today. An anointing is a special, God-given empowering that enables us to serve and honor the Lord in a unique way. An anointing differs from a calling. A calling is the specific purpose for which God created us. Each of us has such a calling. An anointing happens when God comes alongside us and gives us a special empowering to accomplish our purpose in some extraordinary way—something so unique that people step back and say, "Wow, that had to be God!" God's anointing can happen for a single event, over a specific period, or throughout much of a lifetime. While every person has a lasting purpose, God anoints certain individuals for specific tasks or roles that may last for varying periods. God alone makes the decisions of when, how, what, and how long.

Why do I use the term *anointing* to describe this special empowering to accomplish our purpose (or some part of our purpose)? It's a biblical term, more common in the Old Testament than in the New Testament. It typically refers to the consecration of a person or thing to some special (usually sacred) task. Most of the time, oil was poured on the individuals or things to set them apart; they were *anointed* for some special purpose.

From time to time in ancient Israel, God would tell a prophet to anoint some person. The prophet would go to him and pour oil over his head as a sign that God had chosen him for some specific task or role. Moses, for example, anointed his brother, Aaron, to serve as high priest. The prophet Samuel anointed a young shepherd named David to be king over Israel. The anointing meant that God had not only chosen the person to fulfill the task or role but would also give the person the power to succeed in it.

In the New Testament, Jesus is called *Messiah* or *Christ*, in both cases meaning "the anointed one." God anointed Jesus to be our priest, prophet, and king.

Today, every person who puts their faith in Jesus receives special power from God to do specific tasks. The Bible calls these special abilities *spiritual gifts*. No believer needs to worry about missing them! Just work diligently at whatever God gives you to do, and He will supply the gift or gifts you need to accomplish whatever tasks He sets before you.[1]

No one ever poured oil on my head and told me I would become CEO of an arts and crafts retail chain. But early in my career, I realized that God had called me as a merchant to buy and sell merchandise and to excel in it. In the last few years especially, I have become convinced that God has anointed me and my colleagues for a unique assignment. The Lord has empowered us at Hobby Lobby to not only take good care of our staff and employees but also help fund global initiatives that express God's love and expand His kingdom.

Recognizing our anointing doesn't mean we become prideful about it. Anything we accomplish comes as a gift from God. It takes humility to acknowledge that fact. For leaders to remain effective, they must continue to pursue their calling and so be available for God's special anointing.

The Importance of Staying Focused

While we don't follow our competitors, we do visit their stores. I encourage our buyers to ask, What are they doing that's better than us? We can learn a lot from them. In fact, even when I travel I like to visit retail stores. As I do, I learn things and take notes. However, I'll often see many indications that they haven't focused enough attention on what can help them the most. Too many things go on in their stores that have nothing to do with being a great merchant.

Consider just one example, what I call a *cousin*. It is any item that duplicates another item; if we didn't carry it, we would lose very little sales. Suppose that someone comes to us only twice a year asking for a very specific item. More than likely, we don't need to carry it. Items very similar to those we already carry fit into the cousin category. We must be very careful about cousins. Our competitors often carry dozens of cousins throughout their stores.

Vendors make available to us millions of items. At one time we kept eighty thousand regular items in the warehouse, not counting seasonal merchandise; now we have seventy thousand. How could we make such a significant reduction while increasing profits? We eliminated thousands of cousins.

Why should we have six different gold tree stars? We need one, not six. Cousins make our job harder. They require us to have more SKUs (stock keeping units), and every SKU creates more cost. Eliminating cousins helps us to stay focused on what makes us successful.

Keep your people focused on your one thing, whatever it is, whether they work as a technician, a mechanic, or someone in the accounting department. A lack of focus leads to distraction, which typically produces serious problems. I've made this discovery personally.

One day I wanted to do something new. I went to a trade show, saw the merchandise, and said, "What *beautiful* rugs! Oh, I like *that*. And I like *that*!" Our success at Hobby Lobby prompted me to build twelve furniture stores—and my mind quickly went in all directions. I lost my focus.

Eventually I realized I had to get back to who I was. I gave the new venture to somebody else. It was a mistake for me to get distracted by furniture because I don't *know* furniture! I had more than enough to think about just trying to be the best at arts and crafts. That's my one thing.

How to Discover Your One Thing

How do you discover *your* one thing? Let's say that, unlike me, you have more than one gift. Maybe you have three gifts. How do you determine what your one thing is?

It helps me here to remind myself that while the apostle Paul had many gifts, he still focused on a singular mission. God called him to preach to the Gentiles (non-Jews). God told him, "Go; I will send you far away to the Gentiles" (Acts 22:21). That calling defined Paul's entire ministry.

The early church had many needs. The book of Acts describes all sorts of Christians who filled all sorts of important roles. Some served the poor. Some pastored churches. Some served the Jewish community. But Paul knew God hadn't called him to meet every single need.

160

Paul knew his one thing was to preach Jesus to Gentiles, and that one thing drove him all the way to testify before Caesar, the Roman emperor. No matter where Paul traveled, no matter how many years he ministered, he never lost sight of his one thing.

So how do you discover your one thing?

Start with the conviction that God creates us all for a purpose. Ordinarily, He gives us interests and talents that align in some way with that purpose. We'll never find our purpose, however, if we don't first pursue wholeheartedly whatever our hands find to do.[2] God calls us to do our best at whatever we're doing, and I doubt we'll ever find our purpose if we disobey His clear command.

God's purpose and calling for us (our one thing) are bigger than whatever career we pursue to become successful. My calling is to be the best merchant I can be. My focus—at this moment, anyway—is to be the best merchant of *crafts* that I can be. If the craft world crashed and burned tomorrow, I would need to find a different focus, but my purpose and calling would not change. God has gifted me to be a merchant and I know it.

My friend Bobby Gruenewald, founder of the YouVersion Bible app, has lived out this principle. His one thing is technology innovation. Before creating YouVersion—his current focus—Bobby started a web hosting company and then later a fan site. He's offered advice and guidance to other tech startups. Although his jobs have varied over the years, he knows his one thing: using technology innovatively to advance God's kingdom.

I think of another friend, David Jeremiah, founder of Turning Point Ministries. From a young age, he believed his one thing was to teach and preach the Word of God. Since 1969, he has remained focused on honing and developing that skill.

In order to discover your one thing, it may be most helpful to begin by asking what interests you. Where do you persistently gravitate? God probably has given you a gift in that area of interest, so that's where you ought to start looking. Wherever you spend a lot of time and energy, you'll find your main interests. If a thing doesn't interest you, I doubt you'll ever enjoy much success there.

I've known people who have chosen some career path not because it interested them but because they thought they could make a lot of money there. Or maybe they saw a stray opportunity and decided to go for it, even though the thing itself didn't interest them. Such a path usually doesn't lead anywhere appealing, especially long-term.

In a similar way, if you try to do something that you're only halfway good at, it will take you *a lot* more time to succeed than if you had chosen an area in which you already have a good track record. So ask yourself, "What interests me? What am I good at?"

There's no telling ahead of time when you will find your own one thing. It may happen by your twenties or thirties. Or it could happen in your teens or in your forties or even later. But when you pursue with passion whatever your hand finds to do, in time you'll find your purpose. God will see to it. He will promote you. Man doesn't promote you; God promotes you. God will take you from point A to point B because you're obeying what He asks you to do.

Keep in mind that very few of us start out where we'll end up. We just move out and get started, doing the very best we can. Pursue your interests, wherever you're most likely to succeed. I trace a good chunk of my own success to the undeniable fact that I am *totally* interested in buying and selling merchandise.

Keep in mind, too, that although you probably won't end up exactly where you started, you likely will move in essentially the same direction, connecting in some way to what you've already done. While on one level your one thing may seem wildly different, *some* kind of deep connection will exist with your previous experience. I see this pattern in life, and I see it in the Bible. God typically builds on previous history.

For more than fifty years I've worked in the same basic space—retail. I'm not doing now what I did in my twenties, but throughout those years I've bought and sold merchandise. That's where God gave me ability, and that's where I get excited.

I can lose sleep thinking about pony beads. I really can! I know that I can be the best in my field at pony beads. Nobody has better pony beads than Hobby Lobby. We have more in a bag, at a better price, with the right colors—the whole package. Strange as it might seem, pony beads help me to know I've found my one thing.

If you have found success with your own one thing, don't allow yourself to get bored or think more highly of yourself than you should. Don't start adding other pursuits, thinking you can be good at everything. (Remember my furniture store excursion.) Don't let your success take you away from your one thing.

Keep Your One Thing Your Main Thing

When Hobby Lobby began in the early 1970s, we had hundreds and even thousands of competitors in the form of small ma-and-pa shops. Not many of them exist anymore.

At one time, a lot of smaller chains with twenty or thirty stores also competed in our industry, but most of them also have closed. There are essentially only three of us now.

While many of these businesses closed because they lacked the resources to go overseas and buy directly from factories, many of them likely gave up because they had no one thing to keep them focused.

When you know your one thing and stay focused on it, you can become the greatest merchant (or manufacturer or service provider or educator or 501c3) out there. Because we keep our one thing the main thing at Hobby Lobby, we'll always have the best craft department, the best art department, and so on. That's why we're here.

Even though I am Hobby Lobby's CEO, I spend the greatest chunk of my time in marketing. A man once heard about how I spend my work hours and said to me, "That's different. It's sort of like you've sidelined yourself."

Well, what in the world would I do if I spent most of my time every day making sure I had my six or eight key people in place? What would I do after that? I'm the senior vice president of marketing. *That* is my job, and I'm good at it. It gives me something productive to do for forty hours a week. Hobby Lobby buys and sells merchandise, and if nothing gets shipped, no one gets a paycheck.

I've seen what happens when I leave my one thing out of Hobby Lobby's secret sauce, and I don't ever want to repeat that mistake. I doubt we'd survive it.

What's Your One Thing?

Years ago, I periodically went to coffee with a friend who ran a store. Everybody loved him and enjoyed talking to him. One day a customer came into his store looking for a specific spark plug. My friend had a wonderful conversation with that man, but the guy left without his spark plug. My friend didn't have it in stock.

If that customer had come into my store, I might not have said anything to him, but he would have left with a spark plug. The very best customer service is to have the items your customers want in stock.

At Hobby Lobby, we check our available stock at every store every month. A district manager arrives unannounced sometime during the month with a list of one hundred items to check. The store doesn't know when the district manager will show up or what hundred items he or she will count. We've learned that it's one thing to have an item listed on an iPad and another to actually have it on hand. If our one thing is to be a great merchandiser, then we need to have our warehouse-listed items in stock.

What's your one thing? Are you focused on it?

Ten

GET INTO THE WEEDS, NOT THE ALTITUDE

Discussions about leadership almost always emphasize vision. Great leaders, we are told, have a knack for painting such a clear and compelling picture of some desired future that followers not only long to see the vision take shape but also go to great lengths to make it happen. We think of leaders who offer fiery locker room speeches and inspire their teams to great heights. These leaders live in the heights and cast inspiring vision. They remain at the thirty-thousand-foot level and leave details to others.

This view of leadership may be partially true, but it's not the whole picture. Great leaders need to both keep a high-level view and descend into the details. I strongly believe that great leaders need to stay in the weeds.

Starting in the Weeds

When we began Hobby Lobby in 1970, I was working full-time for the now defunct TG&Y. My friend and I saw a trend pop up seemingly overnight. Women had begun making miniature oil paintings of flowers, windmills, and other farm items on canvases and then framing them in small, three-by-three- or four-by-four-inch frames. They pulled the canvas out of the frame, painted a little scene, and reframed it to hang on the wall. They hung these tiny paintings in clusters of half a dozen.

This trend began so quickly that no one in our area could keep up with the consumer demand for picture frames. So my friend and I bought a frame chopper and started making frames. I worked part-time on this new effort while continuing to work full-time at TG&Y.

Two years later, we opened our first retail store of just six hundred square feet. We carried far fewer items than Hobby Lobby stores do today, so I personally made all decisions on what items we would carry. We launched that first store in the heart of the hippie era, when beads had exploded in popularity. Flower children called them "love beads" and used them in necklaces and hemp bracelets. They even made their own beaded curtains to hang in doorframes. So guess what we started selling? Beads.

We filled every spot with merchandise displays. We used every glass container we could find—vases, mason jars, fishbowls, you name it—to display various kinds of beads. Hippies would sit on the carpet and line up their bead designs across the floor, planning their purchases. We knew they stole some beads, but we did the math and realized we would still earn a profit so long as they didn't steal more than 30 percent of our stock.

We have hippies to thank for our existence.

As the years rolled along, I made other merchandise decisions. We tried hard to identify and adjust to the latest trends. Although we don't create trends, Hobby Lobby has always grown by moving with the trends. Whatever craft is trending, we sell the items to make it. This meant macramé in the late 1970s and scrapbooking in the 1990s. We grew largely on trends.

We learned to listen to the customer. The items they bought told us which items we should carry in greater stock. By watching customer patterns, attending trade shows, and reading magazines, we learned to guess which items would fly off our shelves. Predicting trends became easy. As we grew Hobby Lobby, these trends provided our bread and butter.

In the early days, I did most things myself. I lived in the details. When we opened our first store, I swept the entryway and the front sidewalk. I ran the stockroom and stocked shelves. I ran the cash register. We were small enough that I could have a hand in everything. Eventually, we started to add a store every year or so, and I personally opened every new store and signed every new lease.

My wife, Barbara, played a crucial role in starting our company because for the first five years I continued to work my day job. Hobby Lobby would not exist except for my wife. My sons, Mart and Steve, at nine and seven years of age, glued the frames we cut and sold. When you start an organization, *everyone* lives deep in the weeds.

Those early days required me to stay closely involved in every aspect of Hobby Lobby. While the company remained too small for me to delegate tasks to others, I needed to keep my finger on the pulse of everything.

Growing to the Clouds

As Hobby Lobby grew, I continued to try doing it all. We needed more help but lacked the cash flow to afford more employees. We couldn't pay for a full-time person in charge of the warehouse and another full-time person in charge of the stores, so I assigned full-time staff to cover multiple areas. In those days, we definitely flew the plane while building it.

Years into our history, our continued growth enabled us to hire enough help so that we didn't all have to wear multiple hats. Around that time, I heard and believed the counsel mentioned at the start of this chapter, that leaders must fly at the thirty-thousand-foot level. They need to work *on* the organization, not *in* it. They need to see the forest, not the trees. They need to put the right people in the right positions to free themselves to focus on strategy and execution. To our own hurt, I got caught up in these ideas a bit too much.

As we hired more employees and other leaders, I started delegating more. I quit stocking shelves. I stopped ordering inventory. I no longer signed store leases. We had great people running the warehouse, managing the stores, supervising our managers, and acquiring new stores. We had lots of buyers who studied the trends and made decisions about what to put in our stores.

If Hobby Lobby were a ship, we were at full steam ahead. We sailed smooth seas. We had great leaders in place, most of whom had been with us for twenty years or more. I knew I could trust them to run the ship and let me know whenever they hit a snag. They knew what they were doing, and they were good at it. With the accomplished people I had in place, I could have played golf regularly (had I wanted to). I should have felt very happy.

I was deeply bored instead.

I didn't *like* living in the clouds. I needed to get back into the weeds.

When leaders get out of the weeds, very often their organizations already have begun to decline. Bill High reminds me of the rise and decline of Chrysler under its legendary leader, Lee Iacocca. Iacocca took the reins of the struggling company in 1979 and led it to a historic turnaround. He saved Chrysler from bankruptcy and helped it skyrocket to success.

After Chrysler reached its pinnacle, however, Iacocca left the weeds to others. A 1990 *Wall Street Journal* article summarized Iacocca's competing interests: "Mr. Iacocca headed the Statue of Liberty renovation, joined a congressional commission on budget reduction and wrote a second book. He began a syndicated newspaper column, bought an Italian villa where he started bottling his own wine and oil. . . . Critics contend it . . . was a root cause of Chrysler's current problems."[1] Jim Collins wrote that during "the second half of Iacocca's tenure, the company slid 31 percent behind the market and faced another potential bankruptcy."[2]

A great danger lurks at the top! You get bored. You relax. You get out of the weeds. I've seen these symptoms in other leaders. If you are coasting, you might want to consider getting back into the weeds.

I know *weeds* don't sound like an especially appetizing ingredient for a potent secret sauce, but they really are. Think of them like mint—also a weed, but one that spices up our lives. Mint keeps things fresh, just like staying in the weeds.

Back to the Weeds

When I became bored as CEO, I realized I had done too much delegating. In fact, I had done such a good job of it that I lost touch with the lifeblood of our organization. I no longer bought and sold merchandise. I had stopped fulfilling the special role God had given me. As I delegated tasks to others, I also delegated much of our decision-making regarding the buying and selling of merchandise, the one thing that had brought us our success. I didn't realize it, but I had delegated away my calling and the potential for God's anointing.

As a retail business that leans heavily on trends, we grow through the work of skilled buyers who predict what customers will want to buy. Buyers order items from manufacturers (or wholesalers, although in most instances we go directly to the source). The items get shipped to our warehouse and eventually end up on the shelves of Hobby Lobby stores. When I did the buying, I took risks by purchasing trend items in bulk. Most often, those risks proved right.

Back when Hobby Lobby had only one tiny storefront, for example, I bought a truckload of frames—so many frames that we couldn't even fit them inside our store. I set up the trailer in the parking lot, and customers roamed around inside to pick out their frames. Later, during the macramé craze, I took a bigger risk and bought ten trailer loads of macramé, trusting that they would sell. Calculated risks such as these allowed us to make a profit.

After I had largely disengaged from my calling and then struggled with boredom, I began to ask God to give me something big: He directed me back to the weeds, to our layout room, the heart of our marketing efforts. I've spent much of my time there ever since.

Down the hallway from my office at our corporate headquarters is the layout room that replicates a Hobby Lobby store. In it we keep one of each item we sell, arranging all items as if they were displayed in one of our stores. We use this room as the example layout, a model, for all Hobby Lobby stores. I do my best tinkering in there.

On each item we sell, we place a tag that indicates how many of the items we sold in the past month (or quarter, year, etc.), our profit margin, and a few other factors that tell us if we should keep selling it.

While tinkering in the layout room a few years ago, I realized we had a problem with our picture frames. Over time, and probably because of my boredom, we'd gotten lazy. We were buying frames at the wrong cost. At first, I couldn't figure out the real problem. But I prayed and asked God for insight. As I dug deeper, I realized that when we first began—when I was still in the weeds—we'd bought frames based on the linear foot, which allowed us to save dramatically on costs, increase our profits, and give away more money.

Today, I consider the layout room my playground. Most Saturday mornings, I go into work and head to the layout room. I don't have to be there, but I love it. I'll scratch around, looking at all the little tags on the seventy thousand regular items we carry, seeing if we can improve anything.

"If you ever feel like a widow," I've told Barbara, "let me know and I'll come right home. I don't have to be here." But she's normally busy on Saturdays with errands and various outings, so I come to the layout room and poke around.

One Saturday morning, I started going through our twelve departments to locate all the scissors we sell. In the fabric department, we sell fabric shears. In the floral department, we sell floral shears. In the scrapbook department, it's scrapbooking scissors, and so on. Craft scissors. Classroom scissors. Micro scissors. Metal scissors. I found every style of scissors we sell. Some looked so similar that I could hardly tell them apart. They seemed to differ only by the department in which we displayed them.

Monday morning when our buyers arrived at work, I called a meeting. On a worktable I had spread out every pair of scissors we sell. "Why are we selling so many kinds of scissors when they all do basically the same thing?" I asked. "Let's pick the best scissors for each department and get rid of the rest."

We reviewed how many units each pair of scissors sold in a month, noted our profit margin, and then had to decide whether we had too many cousins. Our buyers probably groaned a bit inside at the task I laid before them. It didn't make their job easy! The exercise took a lot of time and energy, but by coming together and getting into the weeds, we learned from one another. We streamlined and simplified the scissor selection in each department.

What are your organization's "scissors"? Yes, learn to delegate, but also make sure you stay involved in the nitty-gritty details. No matter how successful you become, remain engaged in daily functions.

Staying in the Weeds Does Not Equal Micromanaging

No employee needs a micromanager. Staying in the weeds does not mean micromanaging but rather staying engaged with the core functions of your calling and your organization, whatever those may be. But do this in a way that does not burden or dishearten your employees. Stay mindful of the details, but don't provoke constant change. Take it slow and give your team time to adjust.

As I poke around the weeds of merchandising, I see great opportunities with glue, ornaments, decorative lettering, and so on. With nearly seventy thousand items in stock, I doubt I'll ever get out of the weeds. We can configure and reconfigure our items in a million ways to improve our operation and our profitability. And that makes me very happy. My days of boredom are long gone.

If you're feeling at all bored at your job, maybe you need to spend more time in the weeds. You might find something there that, like mint, can perk up your senses and get you energized again.

Make It Better

No doubt you've heard the saying "If it's not broken, don't fix it" or "Leave well enough alone." They mean that if something works fine, don't mess with it. Why chance ruining it?

We have a different motto on our team: "If it's not broken, make it better." If things seem to be going too well, if you are flying high in the clouds at thirty thousand feet, you might want to get back into the weeds to see if you can make something even better.

A couple of years ago we had a record-breaking year for Christmas items. The next year, I encouraged our buyers to rethink some of their decisions. I could have looked at the previous year's Christmas report, noted the highest sales we'd ever had, and said to my buyers, "Great job, everyone. Another fantastic year! Let's do everything the same next year." In fact, they *had* done a super job and we *did* have a record-breaking Christmas season. But by considering what we could do better, we managed to have even greater sales the following year.

Stay in the weeds. You can't see what you need to see if your eyes are always thirty thousand feet above the ground.

It's Not Just for Hobby Lobby

I'm not the only CEO who had to learn the necessity of staying in the weeds. Apple has become a $2 *trillion* company, but it skyrocketed only when its leader returned to the weeds.

Steve Jobs and his business partner, Steve Wozniak, created the first Apple computer in a family garage. Their company quickly rose to success, becoming a household brand for personal computers. In 1983, Jobs hired John Sculley, former president of PepsiCo, to serve as Apple's new CEO. Two years later, the new CEO fired Steve Jobs. For the next twelve years, Apple declined, losing more and more of its market share. After two more CEOs had come and gone, the board asked Jobs to return in 1997.

Jobs immediately dove into the weeds. "We've reviewed the road map of new products and axed more than 70 percent of the projects," he told the company, "keeping the 30 percent that were gems. Plus, we're adding new ones that are a whole new paradigm of looking at computers."

Jobs reshaped Apple's product line and then did the unheard of as a CEO: he started spending all his time on developing a single new product, a new MP3 player. Ben Knauss, an employee who worked on the iPod with Jobs, said, "The interesting thing about the iPod is that since it started, it had 100 percent of Steve Jobs's time. Not many projects get that. He was heavily involved in every single aspect of the project."

The rest is history. As soon as Apple released the iPod, it became an instant success worldwide, eventually dominating 75 percent of the market.[3]

How did Jobs help Apple find success once more? He dove into the weeds.

Jobs had started Apple as an inventor, engineer, and designer. He had a gift for developing new products, and he brought Apple back to its original success by returning to his old role in product development. He stayed in the weeds.

Rarely do CEOs devote 100 percent of their time to one new product. But Jobs knew that the future of the company lay in product innovation. By getting in the weeds, he returned the company to where it could thrive once more.

Get into the Weeds!

What are the weeds in your organization? Do you know what they are? Can you name them? Are you close enough to see them, identify them, and determine what in your organization may need to change?

If you're not regularly in the weeds, have you put so many people around you that you've forgotten about those weeds? Have you neglected something important? Have you delegated away some tasks that need to remain with you?

Stay in those weeds! From there, you can begin to explore new heights.

eleven

CHOOSE SIMPLICITY, NOT PERFECTION

We live in a world of information overload. We have access to news at the push of a button, and if we forget something, we can get a notification on our phone. Those notifications can lead to a confusing mess of choices. The sheer number of choices we have to make can paralyze us. How do we navigate the chaos?

Posted in a warehouse hallway on our Oklahoma City campus, a billboard-sized sign shouts in bright white letters: "Keep it simple. CLOSE COUNTS! Too many choices are harmful to business." It's the only sign in our entire complex with my name on it. I want this reminder front and center as all of us go about our workday.

Information is important, but too many facts can paralyze. Don't give more than what is needed to make a decision. Less is better for you, your people, and your organization.

I personally live out this philosophy by limiting the information I take in. I don't have a cell phone or an email account. I let my assistant field all communication. She lets through what I need to know and filters out what I don't. Beyond that, I don't read any letter longer than one page. When I request reports from our department heads, I ask for a few specific pieces of information, no more. As CEO, I make sure I have hard copies of everything I need to run this company.

I operate this way because I want to run a thousand stores one time, not one store a thousand times. To accomplish that feat, I need to keep things simple.

I'm not suggesting this method for everyone, but it works well for me. However you choose to handle your communication, remember that too much information can distract from the truly important.

Rules . . . with a Few Exceptions

We need a few rules to keep things simple. Otherwise, we can find ourselves choosing a little of this and a little of that, leading to countless disconnected decisions. Without rules, we have only exceptions. And with only exceptions, we are forced to make millions of decisions.

Many people don't even make rules because there are so many exceptions. But I refuse to let the exceptions become the rule. If we have only exceptions, we create a very difficult environment to work in.

I don't *want* to make millions of decisions, so I keep things simple by establishing a few rules. If I ask a manager, "Why did you do this in this way rather than in that way?" I expect they'll have sound reasoning for their decision. If the individual has thought through the issue and has a solid rationale, we're good. I look for consistency and continuity in our decision-making.

Establishing rules requires much more thought and work on the front end, but it saves time in the long run.

Are there exceptions? Sure. What's a rule without an exception? But those exceptions won't stop us from making rules to keep things simple.

Keep It Close

I believe we can do a better job by getting close than by trying to be perfect. To be a perfectionist requires too much information. We need to be close, not exact. And for that, we need close counts. I consider this one of our most important rules.

Close counts refers to approximate numbers, not precise counts. I don't want too much information. This isn't brain surgery where an error of one millimeter could spell disaster. But we do need to keep close counts in key areas.

We operate 1,000 stores (a close count; it's currently about 985, although we should have more than 1,000 stores sometime in 2022), and we need to know the basic quantity of items that we have on hand in each of these stores. I expect our managers to give me these close counts. When you have 1,000 stores and you stock thirty thousand seasonal items as we do, you need to get close. We'll never hit the exact number, so we don't try. We just get close.

We don't sell as many nativities in the northeast as we do in Oklahoma, for example, but we're not going to try to figure out how many nativity sets should go to each store nationwide. If we did that for every seasonal item and every store, do you know how many decisions we'd have to make? Multiply thirty thousand items by one thousand stores and you'll see we'd saddle ourselves with thirty *million* decisions every year. No, thank you. The seasonal items that don't sell get marked down and sell quickly. Because of the way we distribute items to our stores, no store will have more markdowns than they can afford.

We also carry about seventy thousand nonseasonal items. If we didn't have some simple, consistent method for making our purchasing and distribution decisions, the math would instantly get much worse: 70,000 items x 1,000 stores = 70 *million* decisions *every year*. Again, no thanks.

Some say an automated point-of-sale (POS) system could simplify this process for us. A POS system tracks sales through barcodes scanned at the register. If a store sells three items, the warehouse automatically knows to replenish those three items. But what about new items? What about items with no history of sales? And what about stolen items that never get scanned but need to be replenished? We think POS would make things more complicated, not less. Instead, we have developed a simple system that tells us how many items to ship to each of our stores that works very well for Hobby Lobby. It also instructs us how to make better buying decisions—and it cuts down millions of decisions to far, far fewer.

Perfection Not Required

Suppose that in our yarn department, we offered fifty different colors of yarn, but 95 percent of our sales came from just thirty colors. Would we really need the other twenty colors to get that last 5 percent of sales? Know when you have enough items and when acquiring additional items becomes wasted effort. You can save a lot of time and money by being close. You can also lose a lot of money and time by trying to be exact.

For example, Dave Dunn uses close counts in our in-house print shop. Our designers send digital files to be printed. The print shop tries to replicate those files as accurately as possible. But how close is close enough? A printer produces every shade using only four colors: cyan, magenta, yellow, and black. The dots overlay one another to replicate colors. Hold a magnifying glass to anything printed in color and you'll see what I mean.

Dave holds our print shop to high quality standards. Employees work to get every pixel and dot as accurate as possible. But if they get the color dots to line up to 93 percent accuracy, they already have a beautiful print that exceeds the public's standards—and the printers arrive at that level of quality fairly quickly. Dave could say, "That's not enough. We need to get our products to 98 percent accuracy." They could push and tweak the printing press for that extra 5 percent, printing out sample after sample, holding a magnifying glass to each one until the dots lined up just right. But how much effort would they have to spend to reach that last 5 percent in order to reach perfection?

What a waste! Paper lost, time lost, and for what? The average person won't notice the difference. The 93 percent accuracy is still a superior product, already far above average. Dave and his team know when to use close counts.

Whatever you're doing, know the sweet spot. When you exceed the public's expectations and you know you have a superior product, stop there. It's just not worth pursuing that last little bit to achieve perfection.

This philosophy works for anything in life. For over sixty years, Barbara has graciously taken care of our personal checkbook and done a great job. But recently, there started being so many entries that it got more complicated. She made some mistakes I or anyone could make while balancing a checkbook—inverting a number here, missing a calculation there. She would then spend hours trying to get the numbers to balance.

"Barbara," I said, "I think we'll be okay. We're not going to run out of money." We sat down together to find a way to keep it simple.

"You need two things," I said. "First, make sure you have credit for what you've deposited into the bank. That's all you need to know there. And second, make sure you didn't get charged for something you didn't buy. If you know those two things, then whatever balance the bank reports, just write that in your checkbook."

That conversation solved the issue. I haven't heard her laboring over numbers since.

If you're not a brain surgeon, the worst thing you can be in this world is a perfectionist. Perfectionists cause serious problems for themselves.

Instead, choose close counts.

Ratio to Sales

We have given the name *ratio to sales* to the system that keeps our operations simple. It works using close counts. I believe God has given it to us.

Our stocking and buying decisions need to be close, not exact. So instead of making decisions on seventy thousand warehouse items in one thousand individual stores, we need only two numbers:

- The quantity of every item Hobby Lobby sells in a month (that is, how many of each item go out of our warehouse monthly) times two
- A store's annual sales

If we know how many of item A we sell systemwide in a month, and we know how much business each store does annually, then we can determine a close count of how many of item A each store should have on their shelf at any given point. This ratio-to-sales system gives us the close-count numbers we need for each of our stores.

Do we have exceptions from store to store? Of course, but not many. Remember, *keep it simple.* The computer does the math and tells each store how many they should have of each item. It does all of that based on our simple formula.

Again, this is not brain surgery. We're in retail. We want things as simple as possible.

Do you see how such a system simplifies things for us? Instead of having to make one hundred million decisions (one thousand stores times one hundred thousand items), a few simple rules using close counts give us all the information we need. Each store gets assigned their monthly share of every item that Hobby Lobby sells. We call that their "basic."

When we buy a new item for which we have no previous sales information, we find items similar to it and make an educated guess based on their sales. That gets us close enough for starters. Then after three months of tracking sales, we know the correct number to carry. Every store knows how many of each item it should have on its shelves, because that number gets sent out from our headquarters and shows up on the store's iPads.

Every week, each store checks to make sure it has the right number of every item in stock. None of our competitors do that. I admit that such a system might not work in a grocery store that sells hundreds of cans of green beans each month, rather than two units of item A. But in Hobby Lobby's stores, where we sell just one or two each of most of our items a month, it works.

Our system isn't perfect, and we make mistakes. But it doesn't have to be perfect to generate a good profit. What we do works, and our profitability backs up our belief.

Customers Know What to Expect

An old saying goes "I don't want to go around this mountain again." Likewise, we say, "I want to do this once. I don't want to do it again."

As I write, I can tell you almost exactly what we're going to advertise every week next year through December. Why? We keep our ad simple. We feature our bestselling items. The ad's format stays basically the same from week to week. We've decided which items should appear in the ad, where they will go, how often, and at what discounts. Sale items appear in the same spot every week, so customers don't have to hunt for them. We keep everything simple.

When we mark down a seasonal item, we always reduce the price using the same schedule: one markdown every three days, for four cycles. We typically go from 50 percent to 66 percent to 75 percent to 90 percent. Bang, bang, bang, bang. Simple. Our customers know what we're going to do. It's not as though we make new decisions about the ad every morning when we wake up.

Some people object, "But your customers know what you're doing! They'll know they can wait to buy it next week if it's not on sale this week." You know what? I *want* them to know. I might as well say, "Come in next week; I'll have it on sale for half price." I'm good with that. We keep it simple, and it works.

Store Openings

I always err on the side of action. Whatever you do, do it in the simplest and fastest way possible. When we first started opening new stores, we assembled a list of everything that the process requires. Tens of thousands of elements must come together, and if something's missing, the manager knows who to call. Everything is down to a science.

As a result, nobody opens a store faster than we do. From the time we get a store ready to install fixtures (which we manufacture) to the time we open, it takes about two weeks. Our competitors don't come close. We keep the process simple and uniform. Why would we want to do anything more than once?

Ideally, we build stores of fifty-five thousand square feet; everything in the warehouse fits in a store of that size. At times, we can't get fifty-five thousand square feet, so we might have to settle for forty thousand. Rather than squeezing in everybody's departments, we may choose to leave out a department or two. Maybe we put the mirrors on the wall or install the lamps up high.

While a few rules govern how to build every store, every rule needs an exception. For store size, the exception is forty thousand square feet. We never go below that. We dislike creating such stores because they're very tight. Operations doesn't like running them. But we make a good profit out of that forty-thousand-square-foot store. Sometimes that's all you can do, especially where land is scarce and expensive. It's that or nothing. For the most part, however, we aim to build every store the same, over and over. Keep it simple. Know when to be creative and when to stick with what you have.

We have a comprehensive map that shows everywhere we are and everywhere we'd like to be. In time, we'd like to grow to about fourteen hundred locations. And we'll build each new store in exactly the same way.

Where Decisions Multiply Like Rabbits

No department at Hobby Lobby comes even close to the number of choices that merchandising must make. The choices merchandising makes there make us either great or not so great, which explains why we must so carefully analyze all our options and reduce the number of our decisions. That's the domain of the merchant.

My current project is working with our seasonal Christmas sales. For eighteen months I'll spend half of my time working in the layout room. I may say to a buyer, "See this candy department? You can take out half and lose very little sales at Christmas." The additional sales that would come from the extra candy don't justify the space and investments they tie up.

Too many SKUs make everybody's job more difficult. To do our job effectively, we must simplify our processes, not complicate them.

Think of purchasing as a pyramid. First you identify your bestsellers and your slower sellers, and then you get rid of the poor performers and put your money in the top performers. The goal is always to simplify. We want to buy more of the items that sell—those at the top of the pyramid—and fewer of the items that don't. We want fewer SKUs and greater sales, a smaller number of items and more units sold (within reason).

Could we do a better job of serving our customers and making a profit if we had only ninety thousand SKUs rather than one hundred thousand? I don't know, but I'm always eager to find out. So, imagine that I've hired you as my snowman buyer. By conservative estimate, you have thousands of snowmen from which to choose. How will you decide which ones to buy, and how many of each? Here's a hint: close counts.

You can buy snowmen in at least five different mediums: cloth, resin, wood, metal, and glass. They all come in good, better, and best versions and in untold sizes and myriad styles. If you don't have a philosophy that says "keep it simple," you're in trouble.

We know our average customer wants at least one snow-man at twenty-nine dollars, so make sure yours doesn't cost seventy-nine dollars. Let's say you know the cost of each snowman you intend to buy. That's great, but now you must figure out how many of each snowman to purchase. Here's another hint: too many choices are harmful to business. You need only a few for your customer to choose from.

We buy Christmas items over five months, receiving 20 percent of our stock each month, which means that wrapping paper comes at a different time than snowmen. So when should you buy your snowmen? And how will you decide how many snowmen each of our thousand stores should get?

Even when you eliminate all the different snowmen options, you still have distribution decisions to make. How do you simplify your job? You help yourself by using ratio to sales. When you do, all your major decisions on how many snowmen to buy go down to one.

Simplicity is beautiful, isn't it?

Teaching Simplicity

People know me as Mr. Keep It Simple. That's who I am. I want to reduce as many processes and decisions as possible to a few simple rules.

I also want our emerging leaders to know *why* we do what we do, whether in our ads, in our stores, online, with shipping, and so on. I want them to ask, "Why did you choose that? Why did you skip that? Why do you do this every season?"

I'm in the process of writing down basic but crucial information for every department. We don't want to leave a lot of room for guesswork. We want to say, "Here's the rule for you in your department."

But how can I teach anyone to do what I haven't learned to do myself? How can I explain my method of pricing items if I haven't first worked through it myself? Can you see why I spend so much time in the layout room?

Once I solve some issues, I teach and train our buyers. At the same time, they teach me. It's not as though I already have all the answers we need. Together we say, "This works, this doesn't." As a team, we narrow down our choices. All of us want to figure out how to make life simpler.

The Danger of Inaction

More information is not always better. Know what you need to know, and don't get bogged down by extra information.

Fear tends to drive perfectionism. We think, *If I can just control everything, I can keep things from going wrong.* But striving for perfection solves nothing. What's more, it tends to produce inaction. If you keep waiting till conditions are perfect, you'll never launch anything.

I think of Moses sending out twelve spies to explore the promised land. The Israelites had just crossed the Red Sea, received God's laws at Mount Sinai, and traveled through the desert. They camped at the edge of the promised land, waiting to enter. Two spies, Joshua and Caleb, returned full of faith, agreeing with God that the land was indeed good, flowing with milk and honey. God would surely give it to them as promised! The other ten spies focused instead on all the dangers: fearsome giants, fortified cities, powerful enemies. How could the Israelites ever conquer them? They spread fear rather than faith.

The Israelites needed to know how big God was, not the size of the enemy. Instead, they allowed fear to overwhelm them. Perhaps they wanted to wait until they felt battle ready, when conditions seemed perfect. Whatever the case, the people listened to the fearmongers and so refused to enter the promised land, resulting in forty years of trampling the desert. Only after all the rebels died did Joshua lead the people into the promised land. His faith-filled report proved correct.

Know the information you need, and don't worry about the rest. Remember, too much information can be harmful. Move forward in faith, knowing you'll never reach (nor do you have to reach) perfection. Make sound decisions. Take appropriate action. When you make mistakes, own them and fix them. But get rolling!

This piece of our secret sauce tells us that we don't need *exactly* ¼ teaspoon of this and 2½ cups of that to produce what we need. So long as we keep everything close, we're good. Better than good actually. We've set ourselves up for excellence.

The Mighty Sign

It amazes me how often we come back to our sign: "Keep it simple. CLOSE COUNTS! Too many choices are harmful to business." Almost every time I turn around, it seems I apply the sign's message to something else. It keeps us on track and even teaches us new things. Every subcategory of items brings us back to the sign with these three questions:

1. How do we keep it simple?
2. How can we get close?
3. How can we lower the number of choices?

Answering the third question usually accomplishes the other two. By limiting our number of choices, we keep it simple and get close enough.

Could you use something like our sign? Where have you allowed your processes to get too complex? Where can you simplify? Can you aim for close counts rather than for perfection? Where has too much information stunted your growth?

If you need to borrow my sign, do it. Its message has plenty of life left for all of us.

Twelve

GO AT IT WITH ALL YOUR MIGHT, NOT LIFELESSLY

A young man once went to his mentor and said, "I'd love to be able to do what you do."

Puzzled, the mentor asked, "So, what is it that you think I do?"

"Well," the young man replied, "it looks like you do a little bit of business and you do a little bit of ministry. I'd *love* to be able to combine the two."

The old man smiled but said nothing, so the young man pressed in, "How can I do what you do? How can I have that job?"

"All you have to do," replied his mentor with a smile, "is to work your tail off for the next fifty years. *Then* you can do what I do!"

I would have missed my opportunity to lead Hobby Lobby, I believe, if I hadn't given myself fully to the work in front of me, whether it was sorting glass, cleaning up messes, or cutting wood to make frames. Great leaders become great by diligently pursuing whatever work gets set before them.

What lies in front of you? What is your duty? Doing your duty sets you up for becoming a great leader. Do your job wholeheartedly, even the parts that no one else wants to do—*especially* the parts that no one else wants to do. Diligently pursuing your current work sets you up for effective leadership. Doing your job wholeheartedly, as to the Lord, is most often the first step to greater responsibility and larger influence.

Nothing can replace hard work. Too many aspiring leaders set their sights on the corner office, thinking that once they've arrived in the executive suite their hard work will have ended. It doesn't work that way! Profit comes from diligence, regardless of the leadership level.

Don't wear yourself out trying to claw your way to the top. Pursue your current job diligently. Remember that leadership opportunities often start small and then grow as you grow. But if you don't lay the proper foundation, nothing you try to build will stand for long.

And once you arrive at the leadership level you dreamed of, remember that hard work continues to protect you. So many leaders reach the top only to become bored or disengaged. But diligence works as a safeguard against apathy.

With All Your Heart

One Harvard study said that people spend 47 percent of their time thinking about something other than their present activity.[1] Think about that! We spend half of our time distracted, longing for something else that we see as better. We daydream about a superior tomorrow while missing the today that waits in front of us.

The Bible strongly counsels against any such approach: "Whatever your hand finds to do, do it with all your might" (Eccles. 9:10). Paul says, "Whatever you do, work at it with all your heart, as working for the Lord" (Col. 3:23). Elsewhere he writes, "Serve wholeheartedly, as if you were serving the Lord, not people, because you know that the Lord will reward each one for whatever good they do" (Eph. 6:7–8). Proverbs 21:5 declares, "The plans of the diligent lead to profit as surely as haste leads to poverty."

Diligence leads to profit. You can have the best leadership plans in the world, but if you lack a solid work ethic, those plans won't take you anywhere worthwhile. However, if you faithfully work at whatever job you have, God will place you wherever He needs you.

Don't worry about your rank or title. Does it feel as though none of your hard work is paying off? Don't fret. Does it seem that you're descending the ladder rather than climbing it? Don't worry. Focus on being faithful. Keep plugging away. Remain diligent. God knows what He's doing in your life.

"For we are God's handiwork," declares Ephesians 2:10, "created in Christ Jesus to do good works, which God prepared in advance for us to do." Other translations call us God's "masterpiece." God has custom made each one of us for a specific, divine purpose. He has something very definite in mind for you, something He has prepared in advance. He already knows that purpose; He is even now working to get you to that unique destination.

How, though, will you be ready for it if you don't work with all your heart at whatever lies before you *right now*? Whatever job is in front of you, do it diligently. Recognize diligence as the first step to good leadership.

Not Even a Dream

Our printshop manager, Dave Dunn, perfectly exemplifies diligence as the first step toward leadership. Today, he manages all printing for Hobby Lobby, from scrapbook paper to employee applications. When he started his career in high school, he had no idea the path God would lead him on to prepare him for today. As a teenager, Dave got a job at a local grocery store stocking shelves, eventually working his way up to manager. Along the way, he got married and had a son and a daughter.

Dave's own parents separated before he was even born. He never met his biological father. After Dave grew up and became a father himself, he longed to know his own dad. After the birth of his daughter, Dave's mom placed an ad in her hometown newspaper that read simply, "Joe

Smith,[2] your son just had a baby girl." The ad also listed Dave's phone number.

Joe had long since moved away and remarried, but his wife's mother still lived in his old hometown. She also faithfully read the paper every day. When she saw the ad, she called her son-in-law, read him the ad, and gave him the listed phone number. Joe called his son and the very next day flew out to meet him. That meeting sparked a relationship between father and son.

Joe owned a print shop, and within a few years he invited Dave to leave the grocery store industry to help him manage the family business. Dave spent the next ten years working hard with his newfound family and learning the ins and outs of printing.

Eventually, Dave decided to look for another job. A friend of his worked for Hobby Lobby, and since Dave knew retail management, he applied for a comanager position. He soon started working at a Hobby Lobby store in Colorado.

For one of Hobby Lobby's fiscal-year-end meetings, Dave flew to Oklahoma City and toured our corporate offices and warehouses along with our other store managers. After the tour, several managers asked, "What does it take to get a job at corporate headquarters?"

"Go back and be faithful at what you're doing," they heard, "and God will forge your future."

Dave took that advice to heart, and five months later, he received a call from the corporate office. A district manager familiar with both Dave's experience and his work ethic had recommended him for a manager's position in the company print shop.

"Do you have printshop experience?" the recruiter asked.

"Yes," he answered, "ten years."

"Would you be interested in interviewing for the position?" the man inquired.

"Absolutely!" Dave replied.

Dave flew to Oklahoma City, interviewed, was offered the position, and accepted it. Today, he'll tell you that God had perfectly prepared him for his role. We'll tell you that he works wholeheartedly at his job.

We run one of the busiest in-plant print shops in America, and running such a large shop requires expertise. We needed someone with in-depth experience in the printing business—but we never expected to find someone who also had store manager experience. God had divinely prepared Dave to run our print shop even as he worked diligently at whatever God had set before him.

Dave never dreamed that God would combine his retail experience with his print experience to give him a tailor-made leadership position. He just faithfully and diligently worked at whatever God set in front of him.

Diligence before Distinction

Henry Ford exemplified the principle "diligence before distinction" long before he became famous for his trailblazing work in the automotive industry. Before he led a business, he did a lot of inventing. As a child, Ford tinkered with machines to discover how they worked. At age sixteen, he began apprenticing in an engine machine shop, soon earning a promotion to chief engineer. Coworkers described him as "highly proficient as a mechanic and as an operational engineer." On his own time, Ford began playing with his version of the horseless carriage. He kept honing the invention for a dozen years until he finally started Ford Motor Company in 1903.[3] Today, everyone in America recognizes the Ford brand.

Ford's leadership began with diligence. For a dozen years, he worked on his own time, after hours, perfecting his "quadricycle," as he called it. He had no notoriety, no followers, no power. He simply remained diligent at his trade, becoming the best he could be. Years later, his diligence paid off. And even after launching Ford, he continued to perfect the manufacturing process, developing an assembly line in order to mass-produce the Model T. He didn't just settle for early success. The same diligence that began his career carried it forward to greater heights.

If you want to become a good leader, first focus on being a good worker. Don't focus on getting to the top; focus on becoming the best you can be at whatever you're doing—which requires diligence, patience, and faithfulness.

"Do you see someone skilled in their work?" asks the Bible. "They will serve before kings; they will not serve before officials of low rank" (Prov. 22:29). When you're good at what you do, others will pursue you. Working diligently at your job is a first crucial step to leadership.

Many of our best people joined us through entry-level positions and worked their way up, in large part by demonstrating sound character and great work habits.

Our warehouse manager, Bill Woody, first joined our team as a comanager. He worked his way up to store manager and then district manager. He and our vice president, Ken Haywood, once met in Houston, Texas, with Hobby Lobby's district managers. On their return flight to Oklahoma City, Ken said to Bill, "What would you think about running the warehouse?"

"I don't know anything about running a warehouse," Bill replied.

"Sure, you do," Ken said. "You ran one where you used to work."

"I had a twenty-thousand-square-foot stockroom," Bill objected. "That's not the same."

"It's the same principle," Ken insisted. "We'll be in Oklahoma City on Saturday. Let's talk to David about it."

We did discuss the idea, and since Ken had already been working with Bill for years, I approved it. Bill moved to Oklahoma City and started running the warehouse.

Bill immediately felt the steepness of the learning curve. Thirty days after our conversation, he approached Ken in his office after work. "You know, boss, there are easier ways to get rid of me," he told Ken. "You didn't have to bring me all the way back here just to get rid of me— 'cause this place is about to send me over the wall."

Ken encouraged Bill to continue his hard work. Bill kept at it, and soon he got the hang of it. He's remained in that role for nearly thirty years and is still doing a great job. He didn't have that specific skill set when we hired him, but Ken saw Bill as smart, creative, caring, a great team motivator, and a very hard worker. All of these things, working together, make him an extraordinary leader.

No Straight Line to "Success"

One of my favorite Old Testament characters powerfully illustrates the key role of diligence. As a teenager, Joseph had two separate dreams predicting that one day God would make him a great leader. When he described the dreams to his brothers, they instantly grew jealous, plotted to kill him, and in the end decided to sell him into slavery. A group of traders bought Joseph and took him to Egypt and its slave markets.

How did Joseph react when he became a slave? Did he spend time feeling sorry for himself? No. He became the best slave he could be.

Joseph worked hard and God blessed him. He rose up the ranks until he reached the top of his master's household. With Joseph in charge, Potiphar, the captain of the king's guard, worried only about what to eat for dinner. Then one day Potiphar's wife tried to seduce Joseph, who had to literally run away from her. He left his cloak in her hands, which she later used as evidence against him. Despite Joseph's demonstrated integrity, Potiphar threw him into prison.

Does that seem like a great reward for hard work, diligence, and faithfulness?

In prison, Joseph became the best inmate he could be, and God also blessed him there. Only twice does the Bible explicitly tell us that "the LORD was with Joseph": first, when his brothers sold him into slavery (Gen. 39:2–3), and second, when Potiphar threw him into prison (vv. 21, 23). Did Joseph *feel* as though God was with him when he became a slave or when he was thrown into prison? I doubt it. But it is precisely how Scripture relates his story.

One day, two fellow prisoners asked him to interpret their strange dreams. One prisoner got a positive interpretation, while the other learned he would die. Sure enough, the king freed the first prisoner but executed the second. The freed prisoner promised he would speak kindly of Joseph to Pharaoh, but he quickly forgot.

Two long years later, Pharaoh himself had a troubling dream. When he described it to his servants, the former prisoner finally remembered Joseph's special ability and told Pharaoh about it. Pharaoh immediately summoned Joseph. Not only could Joseph interpret the king's dream but he gave Pharaoh a game plan for how to respond to the coming famine that his dream foretold. Pharaoh felt so impressed that he immediately placed Joseph in charge of executing the plan. He even gave Joseph authority over all of Egypt, second in command only to Pharaoh himself.

Overnight, it seemed, Joseph rose from prisoner to prince. But, in fact, it hadn't taken place "overnight" at all. Joseph was seventeen when his brothers sold him into slavery; he was thirty when Pharaoh elevated him to prime minister of Egypt. At no point during those thirteen years did Joseph ever guess that God would use a huge, regional crisis to call him to lead Egypt. Throughout those hard years, Joseph just kept working diligently, as to the Lord.

While in slavery, Joseph served his master with all his heart.

While in prison, Joseph served the warden and his fellow prisoners with all his heart.

Whatever God placed in front of Joseph, Joseph worked at faithfully—and God blessed him for it. Did Joseph ever feel as though life were passing him by, as though he'd missed all his opportunities? He had no way to know that his best years lay ahead of him. He simply worked wholeheartedly at whatever God set before him, and the Lord placed Joseph exactly where he needed to be in order to get him precisely where God intended him to shine.

And God will do the same for you.

Keep Growing through Challenges

I find it interesting that even as Joseph attained the highest rank in leadership his problems weren't over. He learned to lead in times of prosperity, and then God gave him seven years of challenge. People cried out to him for help, and he had to provide direction and hope.

I've found the same to be true at Hobby Lobby. We've had incredible seasons of growth. And in those seasons, it has been fun to see all the changes. But without a doubt, the greatest seasons of my personal growth have come through the challenging times. Whether the possible failure of the business in 1985, the challenge of ownership and succession, or the most recent challenges of COVID, I find these seasons to be the ones in which God stretches and grows me personally.

Those seasons, of course, were big challenges, but it seems that God gives every leader engaged in leading an organization day-to-day challenges as well. These challenges may represent budget issues, people issues, growth issues, or even contractual issues. But I'm convinced that the daily challenges sharpen us and shape us. It's no coincidence that Joseph saw his own troubles accurately. His troubles were meant for a greater good: "God intended it for good to accomplish what is now being done, the saving of many lives" (Gen. 50:20).

Clean Hands, Pure Heart

While hard work is essential, leaders must pair their hard work with solid character. God strongly emphasized that point to me during a business trip to the Philippines in the 1980s.

A year-end buying tour took me to Asia at the same time we were compiling our inventory counts. These reports allow us to see how much profit we have made during a specific period, and until the reports come in, we work off estimates. In my hotel, I received the reports by fax (in

the days before email). I soon saw that we had lower profits that year than anticipated. We still made a profit, but
not nearly what we had hoped for. I opened my Bible and
started reading Psalm 24:

> The earth is the LORD's, and everything in it,
>   the world, and all who live in it. (v. 1)

As I kept reading, suddenly I felt as though the Holy Spirit
began lifting the words off the page and speaking them
directly to my heart—yet another divine episode:

> Who may ascend the mountain of the LORD?
>   Who may stand in his holy place?
> The one who has clean hands and a pure heart,
>   who does not trust in an idol
>   or swear by a false god. (vv. 3–4)

The words "clean hands and a pure heart" resonated in
my brain. The Holy Spirit seemed to be telling me that I
needed the same two things the psalmist had highlighted.

I hadn't been living in sin, dealing dishonestly, or involving myself in anything unsavory. But on that day, I
clearly sensed a divine call toward integrity. God longed
for me to walk in integrity far more than I longed to run
a successful business. He wanted me to deal honestly and
rightly in everything I did, something that was more important than the profit statements getting faxed to me in the
hotel.

I kept reading and saw that the next verse included a promise for those with clean hands and a pure heart:

> They will receive blessing from the LORD
> and vindication from God their Savior. (v. 5)

God wants to bless us, but He reserves a potent kind of blessing for those who have a pure heart toward Him. I returned home from the Philippines with those verses echoing in my heart and a renewed dedication to the Lord in my soul. I wanted to honor Him in my family, my business, and my personal life.

As I reflect over the past forty years since then, I see that without doubt God has blessed our hard work and taken care of us. I feel deeply grateful for His grace, which has fueled my desire to have clean hands and a pure heart, especially as I've witnessed so many leaders get taken down by a lack of character. I don't want that for me or for you.

If you lead while trying to hide poor character—even if you work hard—you hurt your organization, regardless of any great "results" you may have achieved. Poor character will always catch up with you. Character matters every bit as much as diligence, both in your employees and in you.

Do yourself a favor and build a great organization, starting with your hard work paired with godly character. Create an environment in which people feel respected and heard, develop promising leaders-in-training, and hire trustworthy leaders who can help your employees thrive and so achieve more than they ever thought possible.

Sprint to the Finish Line

Do you aspire to broader leadership? Do you want to lead your organization to greater heights? Or maybe you just want to get in the game. Wherever you are, you *must* start with hard work. This, too, is a key piece of the secret sauce.

Are you flipping hamburgers? Then perfect your burger-flipping skills.

Scrubbing floors? Do it with all your might.

Taking classes that seem unrelated to your ultimate career aims? Study wholeheartedly.

As you work hard, in time you'll discover your true passions. And when God puts you in a situation where you can live out those passions, you'll have found your true calling. And by then, you'll be ready.

Or perhaps you're well into your leadership journey. The same concept still applies. If you find yourself coasting along, bored with your current role, set your mind to reengage. Roll up your sleeves, and get back in the game. Whatever you do, work with all your might. The same vigor that propelled you into leadership will sustain you to the end.

I think of Moses as a shining example. God called him to lead the Israelites out of slavery and into the promised land. Moses faithfully led God's people right up to the edge of that land. When it came time for him to die, God led him up Mount Nebo to view the land from a distance. Scripture says, "Moses was a hundred and twenty years old when he died, yet his eyes were not weak nor his strength gone" (Deut. 34:7). What a picture of leading with all your might all the way to the end. God blessed Moses with the strength he needed to get the job done. Moses fulfilled his calling, then he breathed his last.

I can relate to Moses. God has anointed me as a merchant at Hobby Lobby, and I aim to make as much as we can so we can give as much as we can. As long as people still haven't heard the good news of God's love, I still have a job. I am eighty years old, but I haven't retired yet. As long as God gives me strength, I want to stay faithful. I don't want to just coast toward the finish line; I want to sprint. I want to do all that I can, as long as I can, to bring as many people with me to heaven as possible.

Whether you're just starting your leadership journey or have traveled this road for years, God's call stays the same: whatever you do, do it with all your might.

For God's glory.

EPILOGUE

Leadership by the Book

The title of this book, *Leadership Not by the Book*, emphasizes the uncommon business practices that Hobby Lobby has adopted to achieve whatever success we've enjoyed. We don't do business like most companies do, and we believe it's mostly for that reason that God has chosen to bless us as He has.

In fact, though, by taking out one little word, we could have given this work a much less contrarian title while at the same time declaring where our atypical philosophy comes from: *Leadership by the Book.*

As you've learned by now, every one of the ingredients in our secret sauce comes straight out of the Bible. In addition, most of the pivotal moments in our history took place after I experienced some divine episode engineered by the Holy Spirit. Any worthwhile leadership insights I offer, therefore, have their origins in Scripture and through hard lessons taught to me by the Spirit at crucial times in my life. I'd like to leave you with a final insight from *the Book*, hammered into my soul by the Spirit.

Three Keys to Divine Favor

The Lord says to us in His Word:

> These are the ones I look on with favor:
> those who are humble and contrite in spirit,
> and who tremble at my word. (Isa. 66:2)

Every leader must cultivate three crucial traits if the Lord is to bestow His favor on him or her. This trio, working together, also summarizes the secret sauce that has enabled Hobby Lobby to succeed in many ways over the past half century. God says He looks with favor on those

- who are humble,
- who are contrite in spirit, and
- who tremble at God's Word.

The Humble

Many business icons revered today suffered significant failure before they finally succeeded in their chosen fields. Walt Disney, Fred Astaire, Lucille Ball, Henry Ford, Tom Landry, Thomas Edison, Orville and Wilbur Wright, R. H.

Macy, Steven Spielberg, even the Beatles—they all failed in major ways before they succeeded. Some of them learned the lessons of humility better than others! But the best, most successful leaders inevitably learn to be humble because they recognize that, on their own, they utterly lack the ability to create success.

Each of us must learn "I can't do it by myself" before the right conditions can exist to start generating meaningful success. The only way to receive God's favor is through genuine humility, by recognizing how much we need Him. With God, we can do anything He may call us to do. Without Him, we can do nothing.

The Contrite in Spirit

Who uses the word *contrite* these days? It basically means to be broken over sin. God shows His favor to those who come humbly before Him, admitting that they are sinners in need of a savior. While the death of Jesus paid for all our sins, His sacrifice does us no good until we come to Him and ask for His salvation.

A dear friend and colleague, Ken Haywood, remembers well the day he put his faith in Christ. He had responded to a gospel invitation at church by coming forward to kneel at the altar. He tried to get up after a minute but couldn't even move. It was as if God were holding him down. His wife joined him at the altar, and they both gave their hearts to God. "I lost hundreds of pounds of sin that day," Ken told me.

Ken's statement provides a perfect picture of a contrite spirit. It means recognizing you are a sinner and bowing before God in humility until He gives you the strength to get up again. A contrite spirit, coupled with humility, leads to God's blessing, especially when accompanied by the third key trait.

Those Who Tremble at His Word

Imagine you're traveling in a "closed" country. One evening while having a quiet dinner in a quaint, little hole-in-the-wall restaurant, several soldiers burst into the room, arrest you and your party, and take you to an infamous prison. They ask you no questions and give you no details.

Early the next morning, soldiers haul you before a stern-looking judge who tells you, through a translator, "You and your group have been charged with espionage, plotting the overthrow of the government, and aiding counterrevolutionary elements. I have the power to throw you into prison for life, send you to a labor camp, or execute you." He pauses, then adds, "What you say in the next minute will determine the rest of your life."

Put yourself in that fearsome place. Do you tremble at the words of the judge? Or do you treat them like a big joke—smiling, laughing, clowning around? If you're smart, you tremble (and pray!).

Why do you tremble? You tremble because the judge means what he says. You tremble because the judge has the power to do what he threatens. You tremble because your very life is at stake.

Now, take the utter seriousness of that situation and multiply it by a thousand, a million, a billion. When God says He will place His "favor" on those who "tremble at [His] word," He means that He intends to bless all those who count His word as true, who believe Him when He speaks, and who know He has the power, the will, and the wisdom to bring about *whatever* He says He will do.

Do *you* tremble at God's Word?

The Growth That Brings Favor

God wants to give you His favor. He wants to bless you. He wants you to succeed in your leadership. But more than anything, He wants to grow your faith.

More than grow the size of your company, the profit margin of your business, the balance in your bank account, the square footage of your home, and the value of your stock shares, God wants to increase your faith. He wants you to draw near to Him. And when you do, He wants to show you His favor.

If you boil down the secret sauce to one key ingredient, you will find the one element that makes the others work—listening to God and obeying His Word. When people visit Hobby Lobby and exclaim, "This shouldn't work, but it does. Why does this work?" they are tasting the flavor of the secret ingredient: listening to and obeying God.

I *really* want the favor of God to rest on you, your leadership, and your business, organization, or ministry. I've described the secret sauce that underlies most of Hobby Lobby's success so that you can take these principles and run with them to create your own unique, marvelous, potent, and God-glorifying enterprise—something that can powerfully bless men and women, boys and girls, all around the world.

I long for you to experience for yourself the awesome leading of God as He guides you and directs you along new paths to exciting destinations. I urge you to create your own secret sauce, rooted in the cookbook of God's Word and informed by heaven's ultimate chef, the Holy Spirit, in order to bring the love and wisdom of Christ to needy human hearts wherever they may live. You can do it if you partner with the Lord and invite Him to go before you.

Aim for the skies, don't try to go it alone, and remain humble, contrite in spirit, and in awe of God's glorious Word, which is worth listening to and obeying.

Accept that at times, as you listen, the Spirit will lead in ways that seem to make no sense. You might not be asked to go into battle with three hundred men like Gideon or to march around a city seven times at the battle of Jericho like Joshua, but you will face your own tests of obedience. Make sure that you're hearing God's voice and determine ahead of time that you will obey, regardless of the cost and despite any apparent danger. Purposefully call to mind the many instances when He met your needs in surprising, even miraculous ways. Thank Him for His mercy and grace, and ask Him to allow you and empower you to grow your business or organization so that you can reach ever more precious souls for Him.

Where might God take you as you apply your own secret sauce to the venture He's given specifically to you? I don't know, but it thrills me to think of the possibilities!

APPENDIX

Hobby Lobby's Paradigm Change: Moving from Ownership to Stewardship

Guiding Principles

1) **God owns everything.** There are twenty-one verses in the Bible that talk about how God owns everything and how we are just stewards. Below are a few:

> You may say to yourself, "My power and the strength of my hands have produced this wealth for me." But remember the LORD your God, for it is he who gives you the ability to produce wealth, and so confirms his covenant, which he swore to your ancestors, as it is today. (Deut. 8:17–18)

> The earth is the LORD's, and everything in it,
> the world, and all who live in it. (Ps. 24:1)

> For everything in heaven and earth is yours. . . .
> Wealth and honor come from you;
>   you are the ruler of all things.
> In your hands are strength and power
>   to exalt and give strength to all. (1 Chron.
>   29:11–12)

We don't own anything in the world. Everything is God's. It's not ours. It's His. All our wealth was His from the start, He loaned it to us, and it will be His after we're gone. When we grasp these truths, they change how we run a company.

2) **Life is short; eternity is long.** Life is a vapor. We don't know what will happen tomorrow. Eternity lasts forever, and it is the wisest place to invest.

> Now listen, you who say, "Today or tomorrow we will go to this or that city, spend a year there, carry on business and make money." Why, you do not even know what will happen tomorrow. What is your life? You are a mist that appears for a little while and then vanishes. (James 4:13–14)

3) **A man who does not work should not eat.** The Bible is clear that every person needs to work.

> For even when we were with you, we gave you this rule: "The one who is unwilling to work shall not eat." (2 Thess. 3:10)

This mandate holds true no matter the level of wealth. A man who doesn't work shouldn't eat, even if he is a billionaire. If your work makes the world a better place—if you're working for the Lord and not yourself—then work always has value.

Children need to learn the value of work. In parenting, the hardest thing for parents to do is *not* to do. Kids don't need you to take care of everything for them; they need to learn to struggle and overcome. The Bible is clear that children are not entitled to wealth. They must work in order to eat.

4) Wealth can be a curse. Jesus warns us about this in Matthew 19:

> Truly I tell you, it is hard for a rich man to enter the kingdom of heaven. Again I tell you, it is easier for a camel to go through the eye of a needle than for someone who is rich to enter the kingdom of God. (vv. 23–24)

Wealth can take away incentive to work, give us a false sense of security, lure us away from God, and numb our conscience to the reality of heaven. It often makes people more greedy and less generous.

Stock, Say, and Salary

When you think about ownership and control, you've got to address three big issues:

1. Who owns the stock?
2. Who has a say?
3. How much do people get paid?

Stock

If stock gets passed down through a family for generations, you'll eventually have hundreds of shareholders, each with their own voting interest and expectation that the company make enough to support them. There are two problems with this model:

1. When you pass down stock, people receive dividends they did not earn.
2. The ownership gets divided to the point where too many people are trying to lead the company. At Hobby Lobby, no one owns the company. All of the company's voting authority is within 1 percent of the company's stock. The remaining 99 percent of stock is put into Dynasty Trusts.

Say

Who gets the vote? "Few and earned" should be the rule of thumb for members or boards of a God-owned company. Limit votes to a few people who have earned the position and let them have equal voting within the company. Remove yourself from being the singular voice of leadership.

At Hobby Lobby, a Stewardship Trust is set up to hold the voting stock. Five voting members guide the Stewardship Trust. Each member must meet certain criteria. They are interviewed and then sign a document affirming their agreement to the company's vision, mission, and values. These members are not required to be family members— simply whoever is best for stewarding God's wealth.

Salary

No one earns more than what they should. To protect against biases, we have a five-member Personnel Board with equal vote set up to make decisions for all family members concerning work. The CEO should always be part of the Personnel Board whether or not they are family. This Personnel Board decides:

1. If they should receive a given job.
2. If their pay is proportional to their responsibility.
3. When and if they should receive a raise.
4. When and if they should be promoted.
5. When and if they should be fired.

If a family member has a God-given talent for a job, they can be given extra training for that position. But no family member receives money from Hobby Lobby unless they work for Hobby Lobby. Giving children equal amounts is not always fair. If you had an orchard and one child picked two bushels while another picked ten, fair would be receiving what they earned.

The Difference of Stewarding

What happens when you own your company?	What happens when God owns your company?
Wealth is a curse.	Wealth is a tool used for God.
You think the company owes you.	You owe the company.
Ownership creates problems.	Stewardship solves problems.
Family members feel entitled to wealth.	Family members know they must earn their income.
Large concentrated voting authority within one person or a few individuals can be used for personal gain or be handed down for generations without being earned.	100 percent of the company's voting authority is moved within 1 percent of the company's stock. The Green family set up a Stewardship Trust/Dynasty Trust to hold the voting stock. This trust gives five individuals an equal vote to guide the wealth of the company.

ACKNOWLEDGMENTS

At this stage of my life, I have to say that I still love going into work every day. To be honest, writing a book is not something I've aspired to do, but I believe the message contained here is an important one. My hope is that this book will influence millions of people. I take confidence knowing that many people read my last book, *Giving It All Away . . . and Getting It All Back Again* and were influenced to action.

But I also know that completing a book like this is a team effort. I'd like to thank my coauthor Bill High for encouraging me to write this book and pulling together the key players to make it happen.

I appreciate the enthusiasm of my agent, Tom Dean, A Drop of Ink, who was willing to see a publisher even before we'd finalized the proposal. I also cannot thank Baker Books enough for their commitment to forwarding the stories of Christian authors and for their belief in the message of this book. Brian Vos at Baker provided key guidance to our efforts. Steve Halliday and Annika Bergen made incredible contributions to the shaping and editing of the manuscript.

I'm also grateful for the many employees who were willing to be interviewed and share some of their own experiences and learnings for this book. Finally, I'm incredibly grateful for the many CEOs, leaders, and families who have been willing to travel to Oklahoma City for the CEO events we've hosted with Bill over the years. So many of you have encouraged me to write this book and share the secret sauce. Without that encouragement, I'm sure we would not have pushed this ball across the goal line.

NOTES

Chapter 1 Give the True Owner the Vote

1. 1 Chron. 28:1; 1 Cor. 4:1–2; 9:17; Eph. 3:2; Col. 1:25; Titus 1:7; 1 Pet. 4:10.

2. Randy Alcorn, *Managing God's Money* (Carol Stream, IL: Tyndale, 2011), 13.

Chapter 3 Give Away Your Profit

1. David Green with Bill High, *Giving It All Away . . . and Getting It All Back Again: The Way of Living Generously* (Grand Rapids: Zondervan, 2017).

Chapter 5 Build for 150 Years, Not Just the Next Generation

1. Alex Hill, Liz Mellon, and Jules Goddard, "How Winning Organizations Last 100 Years," *Harvard Business Review*, September 27, 2018, https://hbr.org/2018/09/how-winning-organizations-last-100-years.

2. Hill, Mellon, and Goddard, "How Winning Organizations Last 100 Years."

3. Hill, Mellon, and Goddard, "How Winning Organizations Last 100 Years."

4. Hill, Mellon, and Goddard, "How Winning Organizations Last 100 Years."

5. Hill, Mellon, and Goddard, "How Winning Organizations Last 100 Years."

6. Hill, Mellon, and Goddard, "How Winning Organizations Last 100 Years."

7. Hill, Mellon, and Goddard, "How Winning Organizations Last 100 Years."

8. Hill, Mellon, and Goddard, "How Winning Organizations Last 100 Years."

9. Hill, Mellon, and Goddard, "How Winning Organizations Last 100 Years."

10. Hill, Mellon, and Goddard, "How Winning Organizations Last 100 Years."

11. *Britannica*, s.v. "Rothschild Family," by Jean Bouvier, accessed December 22, 2021, https://www.britannica.com/topic/Rothschild-family.

12. "Traditionally Crafted for More than Three Centuries," Kikkoman, accessed December 22, 2021, https://kikkomanusa.com /homecooks/about-us/.

13. Judith A. Ross, "A Taste of Tradition," Harvard Business School, February 1, 1999, https://www.alumni.hbs.edu/stories/Pages /story-bulletin.aspx?num=5421.

14. "Our Founders," Voice of the Martyrs, accessed December 22, 2021, https://www.persecution.com/founders/.

Chapter 6 Drive Family Practices, Not Profit Practices

1. Marissa Levin, "5 Big Regrets That Leaders Have to Overcome to Fulfill Their Dreams," *Inc.*, May 21, 2018, https://www.inc.com /marissa-levin/5-big-leadership-regrets-how-to-avoid-them.html.

2. "Dr. Dobson Shares about His Dad—Part 2 (Transcript)," Dobson Digital Library, accessed September 17, 2021, https://www.dobson library.com/resource/article/ceb838b9-9f1e-4c52-8407-c7e12cede04d.

3. Aaron De Smet, Bonnie Dowling, Marino Mugayar-Baldocchi, and Bill Schaninger, "'Great Attrition' or 'Great Attraction'? The Choice Is Yours," *McKinsey Quarterly*, September 8, 2021, https://www.mckinsey .com/business-functions/people-and-organizational-performance/our -insights/great-attrition-or-great-attraction-the-choice-is-yours.

4. De Smet, Dowling, Mugayar-Baldocchi, and Schaninger, "'Great Attrition' or 'Great Attraction'?"

Chapter 8 Defer to Your People, Don't Just Listen to Them

1. Patrick Lencioni, *The Five Dysfunctions of a Team: A Leadership Fable* (San Francisco: Jossey-Bass, 2002), 202.

2. Jim Collins and Morten T. Hansen, *Great by Choice: Uncertainty, Chaos, and Luck—Why Some Thrive Despite Them All* (New York: HarperCollins, 2011), 139–41.

3. Lencioni, *Five Dysfunctions of a Team*, 202–3.

Chapter 9 Remember Your One Thing, Not the Shiny Things

1. 2 Cor. 1:21; 1 John 2:20, 27.

2. Eccles. 9:10; Eph. 6:7–8; Col. 3:23.

Chapter 10 Get into the Weeds, Not the Altitude

1. Jim Collins, *Good to Great: Why Some Companies Make the Leap . . . and Others Don't* (New York: HarperCollins, 2001), 131–32.

2. Collins, *Good to Great*, 132–33.

3. John C. Maxwell, *The 21 Irrefutable Laws of Leadership: Follow Them and People Will Follow You* (Nashville: Thomas Nelson, 2007), 97–99.

Chapter 12 Go at It with All Your Might, Not Lifelessly

1. Steve Bradt, "Wandering Mind Not a Happy Mind," *Harvard Gazette*, November 11, 2010, https://news.harvard.edu/gazette/story/2010/11/wandering-mind-not-a-happy-mind/.

2. His name has been changed.

3. "Henry Ford's Quadricycle," Ford, accessed October 18, 2021, https://corporate.ford.com/articles/history/henry-fords-greatest-innovation-the-quadricycle.html.

David Green borrowed $600 in 1970 to start making picture frames in a garage. He is now CEO of Hobby Lobby, which employs fifty thousand people at almost one thousand stores in forty-eight states and grosses $8 billion a year. The coauthor of *Giving It All Away . . . and Getting It All Back Again*, Green received the World Changer award in 2013 and is a past recipient of the Ernst & Young Entrepreneur of the Year Award. David and his wife, Barbara, are the proud parents of three, grandparents of ten, and great-grandparents of seventeen (and counting). They live in Oklahoma City.

Bill High is the founder of Vyne Legacy—Family Fruit that Lasts. He is also the founder and executive chairman of The Signatry, a global Christian foundation, and he regularly consults with families on generational legacy. Named one of the Top 25 Speakers in Philanthropy in 2015, High was invited in 2019 to join *Forbes* Nonprofit Council. Bill is also author of the upcoming book *What's the Purpose of Family?* Bill and his wife, Brooke, are the proud parents of four and grandparents of three. They live in the Kansas City area.

Everything You Need to Live a Creative Life

Learn more about the business that launched the Green family legacy.

Helping Families Build Fruit That Lasts for Generations

To learn more about Bill's work and speaking,
visit **billhigh.com** and **vynelegacy.com**.